THE SABBATH

The SABBATH

Which Day and Why?

By M. L. Andreasen

TEACH Services, Inc.
New York

2004   05 06 07 08 09 10 11 12   · 5 4 3 2 1

Copyright © 1995, 2003 TEACH Services, Inc.
ISBN 1-57258-053-4
Library of Congress Catalog Card No. 95-61755

Published by
TEACH Services, Inc.
www.TEACHServices.com

CONTENTS

The Sabbath - - - - - - - - 7

An Enemy of the Sabbath - - - - - 13

The Sabbath Commandment - - - - - 23

The First Sabbath - - - - - - 41

The Sabbath at Sinai - - - - - - 53

The Sabbath in the Old Testament - - - - 71

Christ and the Law - - - - - - 91

Jesus and Tradition - - - - - - 111

Has the Sabbath Been Changed? - - - - 121

Sunday in the New Testament - - - - 137

Some Questions Answered - - - - - 155

Under Grace - - - - - - - - 177

God's Sign and Seal - - - - - - 193

Sabbath Reformation - - - - - - 207

The Final Controversy - - - - - - 231

The Sabbath

THE Sabbath is one of God's choicest gifts to man. It was brought to earth by God Himself, as the crown and glory of the finished creation. Wondrous in beauty must that first Sabbath have been as God, at the end of the six days, rested from all His works which He had made. The heavens were studded with jewels, and the earth was filled with a thousand delights. Earth, sea, and sky proclaimed the glory, and power, and love of God. It would seem that love could do no more than God had done for His own.

And yet God was not satisfied. He had given the earth to the children of men; now He added a bit of heaven. Once a week the Sabbath was to come to earth; once a week God would in a special manner meet with His children; once a week heaven's peace would rest on the whole creation. Coming down from God out of heaven, the Sabbath would descend with healing in its wings, bringing to man rest, peace, and blessing, yea, God Himself. Thrice blessed, it was the golden clasp that bound earth and heaven together, the golden chain that bound the soul to God. As God and man communed together that first Sabbath on earth, the morning stars sang together, and all the sons of God shouted for joy.

But sin and sorrow came in and marred God's perfect creation. Long has evil prevailed, and at times it has

7

seemed that God has forsaken man and left him to his own folly and destruction. From the anguished hearts of millions has ascended the cry to God, How long, O Lord, how long! Yet God has not left the earth, nor man. He still meets with His own; He still sends them the holy Sabbath with balm for the weary, quiet for frayed nerves, comfort for distressed hearts, peace for anxious and troubled souls. For a war-weary world; for hearts that are failing for fear and for looking after those things that are coming to the earth; for bereaved families who mourn the loss of loved ones; for sin-sick souls who long for assurance and peace, God still has a message. Earth may resound with the roar of cannon and the shriek of falling bombs; the droning of messengers of destruction may fill the air; but the sun still rules the heavens; the stars, calm and serene, follow their appointed path; and God is still on the throne. At the determined time He will speak, and will not keep silence. Men shall still hear His voice.

If ever the Sabbath was needed, it is needed now. Amid the tumult of nations, amid the clash of arms, God's voice is heard calling men to worship, to communion, to the Sabbath rest that remains for the people of God. The time has come, and is long overdue, for a Sabbath restoration and reformation. The evil one has almost succeeded in depriving men of God's Sabbath gift, and the church is apathetic. It is time for the Christian, for the church, to awake, and go out to battle for the faith once delivered to the saints. It is time for all to "remember the Sabbath day, to keep it holy."

Two Institutions

Two institutions have come to us from the Garden of Eden: marriage and the Sabbath. Only one of these, the Sabbath, carries over into the earth made new. Of marriage it is written: "When they shall rise from the dead, they neither marry, nor are given in marriage; but are as the angels which are in heaven." Mark 12:25. On the contrary, this is said of the Sabbath: "As the new heavens and the new earth, which I will make, shall remain before Me, saith the Lord, so shall your seed and your name remain. And it shall come to pass, that from one new moon to another, and from one Sabbath to another, shall all flesh come to worship before Me, saith the Lord." Isa. 66:22, 23.

This makes the Sabbath unique. Throughout changing customs and varying dispensations, amid the passing of empires and the crash of nations, surviving floods, famines, and even "the end of all things," the Sabbath stands unmoved and supreme. It, of all institutions, alone abides. Made by God and given to man for an everlasting possession, it endures as eternity itself.

We are not informed about Sabbath observance among the angels; we have no knowledge of what the inhabitants of other worlds are doing in regard to Sabbath rest; but we do know that the Sabbath was made for and given to man, and that Christ claims lordship over it. Mark 2:27, 28. This makes it a divine-human institution, fitted to beings made of clay, but in the image of God, partakers of the divine nature.

The Sabbath

The Sabbath commandment, by its very nature, underlies all the other commandments; in fact, it is fundamental to religion itself. It is the one commandment which provides time for worship, for contemplation, for communion with nature and with God.

Were there no Sabbath, every day would be a day of labor, and life a continuous round of secular pursuits. Nature, as such, knows no Sabbath. The corn grows every day; so do weeds. The storms, rains, hail, observe no Sabbath. Disasters occur, fires rage, accidents happen, regardless of the day of the week. Multitudinous secular duties call for constant attention, and even seven days a week at times seem not enough to do all the work that needs to be done. Were it not for the Sabbath, men would labor every day and yet not get their work done.

But God recognizes the need of rest, spiritual and physical. In the midst of life's pressing demands He calls a halt and bids men cease their activity and give attention to the things of the spirit. To their own astonishment, men find that taking time out for spiritual duties does not hinder but rather helps in temporal affairs; that the physical rest on the Sabbath does not delay their work, but gives them added zest and strength for their common pursuits on the other days of the week. They have found by experience that resting on the Sabbath enables them to do as much work in six days as they formerly did in seven. But over and above any physical gain is the invigoration that comes to the soul through time spent in contemplation, as man in worship comes face to face with himself and with his Maker, and considers the vital themes of life—death, heaven, eternity, duty, and privilege—and probes the depth of his own existence as related to the plan of God.

Spiritual Service

The Sabbath raises man from the level of earthly existence to the plane of the spirit. Six days man toils to provide the needed food, clothing, shelter, and protection against possible contingencies. On the Sabbath he is lifted above all earthly considerations, and communes with his God. On that day he takes his rightful place in creation, lifts his mind to things above, lays aside all that binds him to earth, and enters into the heavenly rest. He meets with those of like precious faith, partakes of the bread which came down from heaven, sits at table with his Lord, and receives his parting blessing as he turns again to his earthly pursuits for another week.

The Sabbath provides the occasion for spiritual service and contemplation. On that day he may consider the marvelous things out of God's law; he may view the glory of God in the heavens above and the earth beneath; he may commune with God and his own soul. Were it not for the time thus provided, man would sustain an irreparable spiritual loss. The Sabbath gives the needed time for contemplation of life and its duties, for God, heaven, and religion. Take the Sabbath away, and the foundation of the other commandments is removed; there would be no stated time for worship, no time dedicated to the consideration of our responsibilities to God and man. Without the Sabbath, life would be an endless round of duties and labor, spiritual things would be neglected, and man's highest end would not be attained. If there is to be religion at all, God must provide time for it. This God has done.

Attacks Upon the Sabbath

From this it can easily be understood that any attack upon the Sabbath is an attack upon religion itself, a thrust aimed at man's spiritual nature. We need not wonder, therefore, that Satan is specially interested in the destruction or the perversion of the Sabbath. If he can destroy it, he has cut a link of communication with heaven. He has sapped the lifeblood of religion, without which Christianity will soon sicken and die. An attack upon the Sabbath is a stab at the heart of worship, at the heart of both man and God.

The nature of the Sabbath makes it peculiarly susceptible to attack from the evil one. It is inconceivable that Satan could ever persuade Christendom that stealing or committing adultery is harmless or permissible. Yet the Sabbath commandment is as surely a part of the moral law as are the others. It is doubtful that Satan could ever persuade Christians that any of the other commandments can be violated with impunity. Yet he has done this with the fourth. How has this been possible? What are the reasons for his success? This will be discussed fully later.

Attacks upon the Sabbath throughout the ages have been numerous and persistent, and they have all been grounded upon human reasoning as against the command of God. Men can see no reason why any other day than one commanded by God is not just as good. Men cannot see why *one day in seven* is not just as good as *the seventh day*. The answer, of course, is that the difference lies in God's command. It is at this point that man's reason sets aside a positive command of God. It is not merely a question of this or that day, but the greater question of obedience to God's command.

The attacks made on the Sabbath have not come merely or even generally from unbelievers or opponents of God. Satan's ingenuity and master mind show themselves in his capacity for enlisting Christians—laymen, preachers, and bishops—in his attack on the Sabbath. Men of learning, men of science, have joined the fray, and the array of talent mustered against the Sabbath is quite formidable. But truth will triumph at last.

One of the most effective and far-reaching attacks upon the Sabbath has come as a by-product of the theory of organic evolution, almost universally accepted by scientists. We consider this attack from the scientific angle the most insidious of all, for more than anything else it destroys faith in the Bible and the record of creation. While a full consideration of this subject does not come under the purview of this volume, it is essential that we give it at least passing attention. This we shall do.

An Enemy of the Sabbath

THE commandment, "Remember the Sabbath day, to keep it holy," rests upon the fact of creation. "In six days the Lord made heaven and earth, the sea, and all that in them is, and rested the seventh day: *wherefore* the Lord blessed the Sabbath day, and hallowed it." Ex. 20:11.

God worked six days and rested the seventh. This fact forms the basis and ground of the commandment. As the Sabbath is a memorial of the fact of creation, it must of necessity remain as long as creation remains.

Evolution disputes this fact of creation by divine fiat as recorded in Genesis. The theory does not provide for, nor admit of, creation in the Bible sense of the word. There are those among the believers in evolution who admit that God might have created the first spark of life which later grew and developed into the life which surrounds us today, but that God created the world as we see it today in its highly developed form, and that He did so in six literal days, is categorically denied. In so far as creation was divided into six epochs, evolutionists reason that these six periods must have been of undetermined length, each probably hundreds of millions of years.

It is clear that in any such scheme a twenty-four-hour Sabbath recurring weekly finds no place. All will admit that if the six days of creation are lengthened into six long periods of time, and if God rested the seventh period

13

—which has not as yet ended, and in which we are still living—there is no possible ground for keeping a weekly Sabbath as a memorial of God's rest. If, on the other hand, we believe the simple Genesis account that "in six days the Lord made heaven and earth," and that He rested on the seventh day, then we can see reason for man's following in His footsteps and obeying His command to rest as He rested. If the theory of evolution is true, then the ground of the Sabbath as presented in the fourth commandment is untrue and irrelevant. There can be no harmony or compromise in these two opposite positions. If one is true, the other falls to the ground. It is for men to choose what and whom they will believe.

The Higher Critics

A hundred or more years ago few had seriously challenged the historicity of the creation record found in the Bible. True, voices here and there had been lifted against a literal view of the creation account, but on the whole there had been no serious challenge.

Then a change occurred. Higher criticism began to make itself felt, while at the same time a new day dawned in science. Without any necessary collusion, the two worked hand in hand to produce a new era in religion—or might we better say a new religion? for this is really what happened. The confidence that had formerly been reposed in the Bible was transferred to science. No longer did men believe that creation had taken place as the Bible recorded it. Science gave a different version, and this version the critics accepted.

The higher critics insisted that the Biblical creation account was confused and not historically true. An editor, they stated, had attempted to put many conflicting traditions together to form a connected story; but if his intent was to make it appear that Genesis was the work of one author, he had not succeeded. The critics had unmasked the clumsy attempt. Not one man had written Genesis, nor two, nor ten. If the editor thought that he had deceived the critics, he was mistaken. They proceeded to lay bare the whole story of the composite authorship of Genesis, and took the editor to task. The story which the critics unfolded was that Genesis was a collection of fables, myths, legends, folklore, tradition, with some little history added, all of which probably had some remote ground in fact, but was so confused as to be of little value as a reliable source of information.

These conclusions of the Biblical critics played into the hands of the scientists and greatly strengthened their case. The Bible account could not be depended upon; this was the conclusion of the critics, and the scientists agreed. The two stood on common ground. Scientists doubted the Bible account of creation; the critics admitted that it was folklore and myth and not intended to be taken literally. Thus the case was won for evolution. The critics joined the scientists, and the case was settled. Both parties pronounced their work good, so good in fact that "there are no rival hypotheses except the outworn and completely refuted idea of special creation, now retained only by the ignorant, the dogmatic, and the prejudiced."—*"Evolution, Genetics, and Eugenics," p. 59.*

What God Thinks

God is patient with men's failings and their ignorances. He knows our frame and remembers that we are only dust. God forgives and forgives, even unto seventy times seven. This is our salvation and hope. God is a wonderful God.

But there are some things that try His patience, humanly speaking. It is not our ignorance. *That* God can bear and even excuse. It is rather our pretended wisdom, our "knowing so many things that are not so," that irks

15

Him. Our hypocrisy and stubbornness, our disinclination and unwillingness to be taught—these try God's patience.

It is not often that God uses sarcasm to express His feelings. There are only a few places in the Bible where it is used, and it seems to be reserved for special occasions and groups. Let us consider one case.

Job passed through experiences that tried him to the utmost. In the midst of his trials he said certain things which he later regretted, and of which he confessed himself to be in ignorance. "I uttered that I understood not; things too wonderful for me, which I knew not." "Wherefore I abhor myself, and repent in dust and ashes." Job 42:3, 6.

God had put some simple questions to Job, and it was these questions which caused him to make the above confession. In asking these questions God had a larger audience in mind, for the principles enunciated hold good under like conditions.

Job had professed to be wise above that which is written. Note the import of the questions propounded by God. "Who is this that darkeneth counsel by words without knowledge? Gird up now thy loins like a man; for I will demand of thee, and answer thou Me. Where wast thou when I laid the foundations of the earth? declare, if thou hast understanding." "Knowest thou it, because thou wast then born? or because the number of thy days is great?" Job 38:2-4, 21.

Note in particular verse four: "Where wast thou when I laid the foundations of the earth? declare, if thou hast understanding." How small that question must have made Job feel! He had evidently discoursed learnedly about what took place when God made the heavens and the earth; and now God asks him where he was at that time, since he seems to know so much about it.

We believe that this was recorded for the benefit of

16

others besides Job. It would be well if a modern disbeliever in Genesis should put himself in Job's place when God asks the embarrassing question: "Where wast thou when I laid the foundations of the earth?" It would make him less sure of his pretended knowledge.

The answer which Job gave, "I uttered that I understood not; things too wonderful for me, which I knew not," was an honest answer. Men presume to know and discuss learnedly about what took place ages ago, and describe events at which they were not present, while they reject the testimony of those who not only were there, but who did the very things upon which these wise men throw doubt. It must amuse God to hear such a display of learning, when He knows—and they ought to know—that their pretended wisdom is only folly.

Biblical Sarcasm

"Knowest thou it, because thou wast then born? or because the number of thy days is great?" The Septuagint renders this: "I know then that thou wert born at that time, and the number of thy years is great." An American Translation, issued by the University of Chicago Press, reads, "You know, for you were born then, and the number of your days is great." The Variorum Reference Bible translates in the margin: "Thou knowest it (ironically), for thou wast then born." Moffatt renders the verse: "Surely you know! you, born when it was made, you who have lived so long!" With these the Revised Version agrees when it translates: "Doubtless, thou knowest, for thou wast then born, and the number of thy days is great!"

This is mild sarcasm, or irony, as the Variorum calls it. It was doubtless intended by God to give the person addressed a truer perspective of himself and of his own importance.

2   17

How devastating such questions would be if addressed by God to a modern disbeliever in Genesis! Where were you, small, puny, insignificant man, who presumes to correct God's version of what He did and how He did it? "Where wast thou when I laid the foundations of the earth?" It would seem that man should be able to learn from this the lesson God intends to convey, and take a humbler attitude.

It must be interesting for God to watch life unfolding, see a little one toddle along amusing himself with a rattle, and the next moment, as it were, see the same individual ready to assume the role of teacher, discoursing wisely about things of which he knows nothing, unwilling to listen to the testimony of those who were present on the occasion of which he speaks. It would seem much wiser to accept the testimony of eyewitnesses than to reject it and substitute nebulous theories. To call such procedure science is to make science ridiculous in the eyes of thinking men. God's one question, "Where wast thou when I laid the foundations of the earth?" should silence forever all profane reasoning about creation which is not founded on personal knowledge or the testimony of those who were present on the occasion and had a part in it.

The Consistent Evolutionist

The Bible knows nothing of evolution. What it has to say of how things came to be is summed up in the words: "In six days the Lord made heaven and earth, the sea, and all that in them is, and rested the seventh day: wherefore the Lord blessed the Sabbath day, and hallowed it." Ex. 20:11.

The consistent evolutionist cannot in any real way believe in Genesis. And not only can he not believe in Genesis. He cannot believe in the Bible as being in any way inspired above other great pieces of literature. The

Bible presents to man a Saviour from sin. But the consistent evolutionist has no use for a Saviour, for he cannot accept of a "fall;" it finds no place in his program. Man did not "fall" in the Genesis meaning of the term. Man is on the upgrade. He began very low and is constantly climbing. So far from "falling" is he, that some declare that if man ever "fell," he fell upward. No, the evolutionists cannot believe in a "fall." They believe in the exact opposite. The very notion that man fell, that in many respects he is growing worse and worse, is entirely inconsistent with their doctrine. They could believe in a fall only as they give up their belief in evolution. The two do not harmonize. Evolution does not provide for a "fall." Hence it does not need a Saviour. Evolution does away with Christ. In this sense it is definitely anti-Christian.

If the creation days are long periods of time, as evolution teaches, it becomes necessary to explain "the evening and the morning" of each day; or, as Genesis 1:16 notes, day and night. There is no way in which we can conceive of a night millions of years in duration, and have any life survive. Furthermore, this alternation of light and darkness took place during each of the six days; hence, if we try to accept both evolution and the Bible, we must conceive of six periods of darkness each followed by a period of light. During no period of darkness that lasted millions of years could vegetable, animal, or human life exist. This consideration alone would rule out any attempt to harmonize the six days of creation with the evolutionary conception of long periods of time.

Adam lived to be 930 years old. The first two days of his life were two of the original seven days; hence they were millions of years in length, if we are to believe the "long period" theory. Consequently Adam would be millions of years old at the time of his death, and not 930.

Men may choose to believe one or the other of these accounts. There is no way of harmonizing them.

Those who believe that the six days of creation were long periods of time, also believe—and of necessity must believe—that the seventh period is also long and has not yet ended, and that we are still living in it. This presents another dilemma for those who wish to be "modern" and believe in evolution without giving up their faith in the Bible. Adam, according to the Bible, did not die till long after the first Sabbath. But if that Sabbath is not yet ended, what about Adam? No one will claim that he is still living. We leave this problem for others to solve.

God blessed the seventh day "because that in it He *had* rested from all His work." Gen. 2:3. How could He bless the day *after* He had rested on it, if that day were millions of years in length and has not yet ended? God could bless the day *after* He had rested on it only if those days were ordinary days. If they were not, the whole record falls to the ground.

Considerations and objections such as these could be extended at great length. We have presented these for the one purpose of showing that there is no way in which the Biblical account and the theory of evolution can be harmonized. Men must choose between one or the other. Both cannot be true.

Our Position

It is not to be supposed that the statements here made are meant to constitute a wholesale condemnation of the adherents of the evolution theory. Far from it. We believe that there are thousands and even millions of sincere, honest Christians who are tainted with this destructive philosophy. Without thinking things through, they adhere to certain beliefs, having faith that their leaders know even if they themselves do not, and that surely the leaders will not lead them astray. There are doubtless multitudes who are not consistent evolutionists, and do not realize the implications of their belief. All this, however, does not in the least alter the fact that evolution as it is being taught and believed today constitutes one of the most serious challenges to Bible Christianity, a challenge that must be met or Christianity is doomed. And with this the Sabbath is closely bound up. If evolution is true, there is no Sabbath, and no need of any.

It is clear from what has been presented that there can be no agreement between belief in the Bible and belief in the evolutionary theory. The one is destructive of the other. No man can believe in the word of God and also believe in evolution. They are mutually exclusive. It is impossible to straddle the question as many attempt to do. It must be either, or. It cannot be both.

In saying all this, we do not cast reflection upon the findings of science as such. Facts are facts by whomsoever found and propagated. Bible believers do not deny facts. They believe the facts as much as their most stanch evolutionary friends do. What they object to is the arrangement—and even manipulation—of facts to bolster an anti-Christian and anti-Biblical theory. Science has a right and a duty to find and present facts. That is its legitimate field. But when science enters the field of religion; when it arranges its facts so that it becomes destructive of faith and religion; when it definitely challenges revealed truth and sets itself in opposition to the Bible, ridiculing those who still adhere to a "Thus saith the Lord," then it ceases to be science and becomes an anti-Christian force and influence to whom no quarter should be given and from whom none should be asked.

The Sabbath Commandment

"Remember the Sabbath day, to keep it holy. Six days shalt thou labor, and do all thy work: but the seventh day is the Sabbath of the Lord thy God: in it thou shalt not do any work, thou, nor thy son, nor thy daughter, thy manservant, nor thy maidservant, nor thy cattle, nor thy stranger that is within thy gates: for in six days the Lord made heaven and earth, the sea, and all that in them is, and rested the seventh day: wherefore the Lord blessed the Sabbath day, and hallowed it." Ex. 20:8-11.

The first word in this commandment, "remember," sets it apart from the other commandments and lends it distinction. When God gave the Sabbath to man, He knew the great value of His gift, and He also knew of the widespread disregard into which it would fall. He knew that Satan would use this commandment as his special point of attack upon the church, and would do everything in his power to cause men to forget the Sabbath. He knew that in time men would lose the sense of the sacredness of the day, and ignore its binding obligation. For these reasons God called special attention to the Sabbath when He announced the law at Sinai, and asked that it be particularly kept in mind. All the commandments of God are vital, and none is to be neglected. But to one He gave distinction above the rest, asking His people not to forget it.

Because of its unique character, this commandment has been broken—by saint and sinner alike—more than any

23

other commandment. Men who would never think of being dishonest or telling a falsehood, who would never knowingly break any of the other commandments, think nothing of breaking the Sabbath of the Lord. They ignore entirely the fact that the Lord blessed this day above other days, that He made it for and gave it to man, and that He has never revoked the blessing with which He once invested it, nor has He taken back His gift. Men forget that in rejecting the gift, they wound the Giver.

Sabbathkeeping is vital to Christianity. Not without cause did God choose one day of the seven and set it apart for spiritual exercises. He knew that man needed a definite time for worship, a day when he could lay aside the cares of this life and turn his thoughts to heaven and home.

This, of course, would specially be the case after man fell. Driven out of his Eden home, unable to walk in the garden and talk with God as he had formerly done, compelled to earn his bread in the sweat of his face, man needed one day when he might cease toiling and prepare his soul for communion with God. Without the Sabbath all would be labor and sweat without respite, every day would be alike, and there would be a continual awareness of separation from God. But the arrival of the Sabbath brought renewed hope, joy, and courage. It gave opportunity for communion with God, and was prophetic of the time when heaven and earth should once more be united.

He who takes the Sabbath away, takes worship away, closes one of the doors to heaven, and greatly impoverishes spiritual life. The Sabbath stands for worship, meditation, reflection, study, prayer, communion, fellowship. If any of these are neglected or seriously interfered with, religion ceases to be effective, and worldliness takes the ascendancy. For this reason Satan considers the overthrow of the Sabbath one of his best means of causing men to forget God, and of lowering the spiritual tone of the people. As men forget the Sabbath, they forget God. As they become careless in Sabbathkeeping, they become careless in other religious duties. Sabbathkeeping is an accurate barometer of spiritual life.

Basis of the Fourth Commandment

The Sabbath commandment rests solely on a "Thus saith the Lord," and is not in the unregenerate man buttressed by an approving or accusing conscience. Such commandments as "Thou shalt not kill" and "Thou shalt not steal" have conscience on their side. While there may be tribes and individuals who have little knowledge of the respect for these commandments, the normal individual has feelings of ill desert as he transgresses them. But this is not ordinarily the case with Sabbath desecration, at least not until special revelation or light comes to the individual. The non-Christian finds it hard to understand why work done on one day of the week is commendable, while the same work done on another day is reprehensible; why one day a thing is right and commendable, and on another day the same thing is sin. He does not see that the difference is not in the thing done, but in the time when it is done. He can find no ground for such difference in nature or science. To him it appears illogical and arbitrary.

The Christian likewise can find no ground for Sabbathkeeping in nature. The stars move in their appointed path regardless of the Sabbath; the corn grows; the trees yield their meat; the animal creation is unaware of any day of rest; the rains come and the sun shines—all with no discernible difference in days. Nature has no Sabbath as such and does not point to any. Why, then, should man keep the Sabbath? To the Christian there is only one reason, and no other; but that reason is enough: God has

25

spoken. The Sabbath commandment rests definitely and solely on a "Thus saith the Lord," and has no ground in nature, as such. It is for this reason that God makes the Sabbath His sign and test. This will be discussed later.

When Satan attacks the Sabbath, he attacks a commandment that in a special sense is based upon and predicates faith in God. If he can win here, the victory indeed is great. If he can secularize the day, he has taken away from the Christian the hour of communion and prayer, the hour of study and peace, the hour when he can meet with others of like precious faith for mutual encouragement and edification. He has taken away a vital link in the chain that binds heaven and earth together.

The Sabbath of the fourth commandment supplies time for the consideration of the things of the spirit. Men do not attend to religious duties unless a specific time is set apart for that purpose. There are a multitude of things that continuously call for attention, and every day of the week could profitably be used for purely secular affairs; and this would be done, were it not for the fact that God calls men to remember the Sabbath day to keep it holy. The Sabbath is a weekly call to come back to God, to turn away from the things of the world, and to give attention to the spirit. Satan knows the value of the Sabbath to religion, and he is not slow to improve every opportunity to destroy it. If he can make the Sabbath of none effect, he has not only destroyed holy time, but has frustrated one of the great means of grace, and deprived man of the Sabbath blessing.

Breaking the fourth commandment is not like breaking some of the other commandments. One man may kill another in a fit of anger; he may rashly take the name of God in vain; or he may suddenly be overcome by a great passion. But not so with failure to keep the fourth commandment. Sabbathbreaking does not have the excuse of sudden passion or of inordinate desire. It is not like a great sin or a destructive habit. It is rather a symptom of spiritual decline, of departure from God, of estrangement from the promise, of a sickly Christian experience. Let this be emphasized: it is a symptom indicative of disease, and reveals an inward condition of apostasy from God. Its roots lie deeper than the apparent transgression. It signalizes a departure from spiritual life and holy living, and presages the separation of the soul from God. Sabbathkeeping is a spiritual barometer, a sign of sanctification, a gauge of our friendship and fellowship with God.

While Sabbathbreaking is a symptom, it is also a disease. It fosters irreligion and encourages disobedience in other respects. It starves the soul and weakens it, deprives man of the means of spiritual sustenance, and makes him susceptible to coarser temptations. It is one of Satan's shrewdest inventions. In this he can get the support of a large portion of Christendom, which would not be possible with any other commandment. Men do not understand as they should, that the Sabbath is one of the chief channels of communication with God, that breaking the Sabbath breaks the connection with heaven and shuts off the stream of spiritual life. They do not understand that "the Sabbath is a golden clasp that unites God and His people."

The Place of the Sabbath

The Sabbath commandment occupies an interesting position in the law of God. Three great commandments that deal with God precede it, and six that deal with man follow it. The Sabbath command belongs to both tables of the law, and partakes of the nature of both. It has a Godward and a manward aspect. It is God's Sabbath, but we, men, are to keep it. It commands worship, and also work. It combines in a unique way the sacred and the common, outlining our duty to God and man. It divides all time into secular and holy time, and defines man's duty to each. It commands labor and it commands rest, giving to each its allotted share in the plan of God.

Men need a Sabbath. The world is too much with us. We are rushed with so many things that we fail to take time to think. We have no leisure, no time for spiritual exercise, no time for study, reflection, or meditation, only as we deliberately set aside a time for it. This God wants us to do. And He wants us to choose the time He has chosen. He wants us to "remember the Sabbath day, to keep it holy."

As it would be quite impossible for a little girl to keep her dress clean if she began to play in the mud and got her hands soiled, so it is quite impossible for us to keep the day holy unless we refrain from sin and evil and all that defiles. If her little hands were soiled, it would not be long until her dress would be soiled. The only hope of keeping her dress clean would be to stay away from all that is unclean—all that defiles. Only as she kept herself clean, could she keep her garments clean.

The parallel is plain. God's Sabbath day is holy. It is a sanctified day. It is God's holy rest. We are not to regard it lightly. We are not to trample it underfoot. We are not to do our own pleasure on it. We are not to speak our own words. We are not to pollute it. We are to keep it holy. Isa. 58:13; Eze. 20:13, 21. This can be done only as we ourselves are holy and keep away from all that defiles and pollutes.

The Six Days

"Six days shalt thou labor." This statement is part of the Sabbath commandment, and is vital. The commandment enjoins not only rest, but also labor. Just as surely as we are to rest on the Sabbath day, we are to labor the other six. The Sabbath commandment covers all time, all seven days of the week.

Some people stress that part of the commandment that deals with rest, and forget the other part that deals with labor. But the one is as binding as the other. No man can be a Christian and be indolent. No man can keep the Sabbath unless he is also willing to work. The two ideas go together, and it takes both to make the Sabbath commandment.

The true Christian is industrious. He does not unnecessarily "live on" his relatives or friends. He does not arrange to do all his visiting at mealtime. He does not give broad hints in regard to his needs, so as to arouse sympathy. He does not expect a reward for every little service he performs. He does not fawn upon the rich or despise the poor. He does not demand special concessions. He pays his bills, and pays them promptly. He does not need a supervisor to make sure that he does his work. He does not become industrious when his superior observes him, and slacken his work immediately after he is left alone. He does more than he is paid for. He is no shirker. He is not an expert at alibis. He is always willing, and when a task is done, he asks for another. He can see work to be done, and does it, or offers his services. He can be found where help is needed, and does not always have pressing business elsewhere. He gives liberally of his time, and is cheerful about it. He knows his business, but is willing to learn. He is never satisfied with slipshod work. He is as careful of his work as he is of his religion.

The true Christian is such a man. He is in demand everywhere. It is hard to find him idle. If he loses one position, he gets another. If he loses that, he makes a place for himself. He is resourceful and energetic. God and men are proud of him.

Recreation

Must a man work six days of every week? May he never take a vacation? If the commandment said only, "Six days shalt thou labor," the question might be debatable. But this is added: "and do all thy work." We are to do all our work. If it takes all six days to do it, we are to work six days. But if we can do our work in five days, or four, or three, we need not work six. The point is, we are to get our work *done*. We are not to shirk or leave our task unfinished while we go pleasure seeking. "Six days shalt thou labor, and do all thy work." We may not work on the Sabbath. That day we are to rest. But we are to plan our work in such a way that we will get it done in six days. This God demands.

Some people do not like the sound of the word "labor." Work is distasteful to them, and labor is even worse. It smacks of the soil, or toil, or pain. Even so. Labor may be hard. Labor may be wearisome. Labor may be monotonous. But it is God given, and is for our good. In a sinful world we can thank God for labor. In certain respects, it is our salvation. Only he who has labored can appreciate rest.

A great deal is said in the Bible about work. This is as it should be. We all need to have impressed upon our minds not only that we have *a* work to do, but that we have *work* to do. Paul did a wonderful work. And while he did this work, he worked at his daily task. He neglected neither. This is an example for such as think themselves too good or too important to do ordinary work. Many a young girl who thinks it would be romantic to work for the heathen in Africa, would frown at the suggestion that in the meantime she might help her mother with the dishes. It does not occur to her that the one thing may be a preparation for the other.

Sabbath Rest

"Six days shalt thou labor, and do all thy work: *but—*" Note that "but." It is well to work, *but*. Some are so interested in work that they cannot stop. Work is their life. From early morning till late at night they are working. They hardly take time to eat or sleep. With them it is work, work, and only work. They have little patience with anyone who does not follow their example. They have no time to go to church, no time for worship, no time for study or recreation; they only work, work, work.

To such God says: "It is well that you work, *but* you must not forget that I have other claims upon you. Work is not all. I have appointed a day upon which you are not to do your own work. On that day you are to rest and refresh yourself. You are to turn away from secular things and commune with Heaven. You are to remember the Sabbath day to keep it holy. It is My day, and I want you to share My rest."

With some, even with so-called Christians, Sabbath-keeping has fallen into disrepute. Sabbathkeeping is in their minds associated with the "old Jewish Sabbath," or perhaps with the "Puritan Sabbath," or with some unfortunate experience which they had as children, when they were not permitted so much as to stir upon the Sabbath. Let such remember that when the evil one cannot hinder, he sometimes pushes too far, and that true Sabbathkeeping is one of the greatest blessings which God has given to mankind. As stated before, this is one reason Satan is anxious to destroy both the Sabbath and Sabbathkeeping; and he has succeeded to an astonishing extent.

The reason given in the commandment for observing the Sabbath is not merely our physical well-being, as is popularly supposed. It is indeed true that man requires physical rest to refresh his body. But needful as such rest may be, *that* is not the reason given in the commandment. The reason there given is the example of God. He rested, and so we are to rest. Note the wording: "Six days shalt thou labor, and do all thy work: but the seventh day is the Sabbath of the Lord thy God: . . . for in six days the Lord made heaven and earth, . . . and rested the seventh day." That is: God worked, and therefore we are to work; God rested, and therefore we are to rest. It is a matter of example; only later did it become a matter of command. Example is enough; that is what Adam had in the Garden of Eden. Later, because of laxity, it became necessary to add the command.

The Sabbath command is the only commandment in the observance of which God could join man. It would be highly improper to speak of God as keeping the first commandment, "Thou shalt have no other gods before Me." So it is with the second and the third. Again, it would be highly irreverent to speak of God as keeping the last six commandments. A moment's reflection will make this clear. Stealing, lying, adultery, all these have no place with reference to God. But there is one commandment in the observance of which God could join man: the Sabbath commandment. Man can keep it; God can keep it. Thus the Sabbath is the meeting place of God and man. In the Garden of Eden divinity and humanity joined in its observance. It was the golden clasp that united heaven and earth then; it will again serve that purpose in the earth made new. When God deigned to come to this earth and meet with Adam and Eve, He instituted the Sabbath, blessed and sanctified it, and gave it as a gift to man. The Sabbath is a bit of heaven, God's own gift. Let us take heed, lest we refuse this blessed gift of God.

"The Sabbath was made for man," and was "to be a sign between Me and them, that they might know that I am the Lord that sanctify them." Ex. 20:10; Mark 2:27;

Eze. 20:12. On this basis He invites us to join Him in His regard for the Sabbath, and promises that those "that keep My Sabbaths, and choose the things that please Me, and take hold of My covenant: even unto them will I give in Mine house and within My walls a place and a name better than of sons and of daughters: I will give them an everlasting name, that shall not be cut off." Isa. 56:4, 5. No promise could be of wider import or of greater significance. It indicates strongly what has been mentioned before, that true Sabbathkeeping is indicative of holiness of life, of sanctification, of communion with God, and that the Lord considers it a sign of union with Him.

The Observance of the Sabbath

In regard to the outward observance of the Sabbath, what does the Lord require? First, "In it thou shalt not do any work." This is defined to refer to our own work and pleasure. "If thou turn away thy foot from the Sabbath, from doing thy pleasure on My holy day; and call the Sabbath a delight, the holy of the Lord, honorable; and shalt honor Him, not doing thine own ways, nor finding thine own pleasure, nor speaking thine own words: then shalt thou delight thyself in the Lord; and I will cause thee to ride upon the high places of the earth, and feed thee with the heritage of Jacob thy father: for the mouth of the Lord hath spoken it." Isa. 58:13, 14. Note the words: "Not doing thine own ways, nor finding thine own pleasure, nor speaking thine own words." This, then, forbids selfish observance of the day; it forbids using it as a day to please ourselves. This is the negative side of the commandment.

For the positive observance of the day, we must go to the example of our Lord and Saviour when He was here on earth. Christ is "Lord also of the Sabbath." Mark 2:28. "All things were made by Him; and without Him was not

3

anything made that was made." John 1:3. If "all things" were made by Christ, if the Sabbath "was made" (Mark 2:27), then Christ made it. Being thus closely connected with it, He knows how it should be observed, and we may safely follow His example. He will not lead us astray.

How did Christ observe the day? "As His custom was, He went into the synagogue on the Sabbath day." Luke 4:16. Christ went to church on the Sabbath. This was no spasmodic or occasional attendance. It was "His custom" to do so. He had a part in the service. He "stood up for to read." It was the custom in those days to invite those who were capable of reading or speaking to lead out in the service. Christ did not draw back when He was so invited. He stood up to read.

But Christ did more than go to church on the Sabbath. He went about doing good. He healed and helped wherever He could. Often, upon coming out of the synagogue, He would accept an invitation to go to a home, as in the instance recorded in Luke 4:38, 39. On that occasion "He arose out of the synagogue, and entered into Simon's house." Here He found one sick, "taken with a great fever." "And He stood over her, and rebuked the fever; and it left her."

At times this healing was done in the synagogue itself. On one occasion there was a man with a withered hand, and His enemies "watched . . . whether He would heal him on the Sabbath day." Mark 3:1-5. They did not have long to wait. To the man He said: "Stretch forth thine hand. And he stretched it out: and his hand was restored whole as the other."

The Pharisees

It was at this time that Christ asked a question which throws light on the meaning of true Sabbathkeeping. The

Pharisees were watching Him. He knew that they were ready to take "counsel with the Herodians against Him, how they might destroy Him." Mark 3:6. But He had a work to do. He must be true to Himself and to His God, though it might mean losing His life. So "He saith unto them, Is it lawful to do good on the Sabbath days, or to do evil? to save life, or to kill? But they held their peace."

The Sabbathkeeping of the Pharisees was mostly negative. They had numerous rules in regard to what must not be done. With them it was always, You must not do this; you must not do that. Christ was positive. His conclusion was, It is lawful to do good on the Sabbath day.

Christ walked in the fields on the Sabbath. On one of these occasions He was accosted by the Pharisees with the charge that He was permitting His disciples to do that which was not lawful. Mark 2:23-28. We may rightly draw the conclusion from this and other incidents that Christ did not keep the Sabbath in the approved Pharisaical manner. He went about doing good; He healed and helped. He made the Sabbath a day of joy and happiness, rather than a day of gloom and repression.

That Christ was a profound student both of Scripture and of nature is evident from the respect which His knowledge commanded even at an early age. Luke 2:41-52. In His sermons and teachings He made frequent reference to nature and to the things of nature. Such knowledge could have come to Him only through constant study, reflection, and observation. Is it too much to believe that when His week's work as a carpenter was done, He went out to commune with nature and nature's God, to reflect, meditate, study, and pray? Is it too much to believe that here is where He received His intimate acquaintance with the scroll of the prophets as well as with nature?

It is significant that "He found the place" for which He was looking in the book of Isaiah. Luke 4:17. He

35

was using the synagogue copy of the Scriptures, but He was sufficiently familiar with the writings to be able to find what He wanted. Not all can do this, and some ministers might even have difficulty. While we would not draw unwarranted conclusions from this incident, we know that Christ was acquainted with the Scriptures in a definite way. As He worked at His trade from day to day, the Sabbath was ordinarily the only day in which He could uninterruptedly do such study. We are safe in assuming that part of the Sabbath was used by the Lord in making Himself better acquainted with the writings of old, and that He did such thorough work that He was more than ordinarily well read.

Christ's Sabbathkeeping

When we sum up what we know concerning the manner in which Christ spent the Sabbath, we find that He went to church, that He preached and healed, that He took walks in the fields, that He studied, prayed, and meditated. If we were to venture an opinion regarding how this time was divided, we would not be on sure ground. Evidently a change came with His entrance upon His public ministry. After that, much prominence is given to His going about doing good and healing. In any event, Christ was not a recluse, keeping to Himself and withholding from the world His presence and His service. He loved to mingle with the people. He even accepted invitations on the Sabbath to dine with Pharisees where others were present, and He used these occasions to bring out some of His most pertinent lessons for them and for all.

We need to be careful, lest we go to extremes. We must carefully guard the Sabbath, so that it does not degenerate into a day of recreation and relaxation only. The Sabbath is not a day for excursions and travel. It is not a day for sight-seeing and merrymaking. It is a day of solemn convocation and worship, a day of prayer and of seeking God. No one should needlessly absent himself from worship on that day. It may be that there is some distance to travel in order to meet with church members, it may be inconvenient and tiresome to get to the place where God's people assemble for worship, but we believe that every reasonable effort should be made to be there, and that God not only permits us to make such effort, but is pleased to have us do so. The Sabbath is first of all a day of worship, a day on which God's people assemble to hear the word and to tell of their own experiences and be encouraged by the report of others. As far as possible, all should be in their appointed place when the hour of worship comes.

After the service, it is not necessary, in order to observe the Sabbath according to the commandment, to stay indoors. Christ accepted invitations on the Sabbath, and spent at least a part of the time in conversation and teaching. But He did more than that. He spent much time in going about doing good. So may we. There is no reason why the Sabbath should not be a day of visiting the sick and the shut-ins, of bringing cheer to those on beds of sickness, of visiting homes for crippled children, for the aged, for the unprivileged and unfortunate, of sending messages and flowers to the lonely, and in general of doing that which Christ Himself would delight to do were He here. A Sabbath spent in this way would not only be a blessing to the person who does the work, but would react in a thousand ways to further the cause of Christianity, in making practical that which is preached from the pulpit, but which too often is not translated into acts. To follow Christ's way of Sabbathkeeping would make the Sabbath a day of blessing and delight to a large number of people who might not have the gospel preached to them in any other way.

Viewed from the angle of Christ's manner of Sabbath-keeping, the day should be one of the preaching of the gospel both by word of mouth and by way of practice. The Sabbath should be a demonstration of the gospel in operation. When God commands us to remember the Sabbath day to keep it holy, He is in that command providing not only for the observance of a day for our benefit, but also for giving the world an object lesson in applied Christianity. The Sabbath was given not only *to* man, but *for* man. Rightly observed and used, it should be a mighty means for the proclamation of the true gospel in a way which all can understand. As Christ was the word made flesh, so the Sabbath is heaven transplanted, a day given to man as a reminder of that which once was and which again shall be. It came from God, and it is to be given back to Him again in service.

Practical Applications

The command to observe the Sabbath extends to children, servants, and strangers that are within our jurisdiction. The reading of the command is, "The seventh day is the Sabbath of the Lord thy God: in it thou shalt not do any work, thou, nor thy son, nor thy daughter, thy manservant, nor thy maidservant, nor thy cattle, nor thy stranger that is within thy gates." Ex. 20:10.

A vital principle is here involved. We are responsible for ourselves, and also for those who are within our gates. We are not only to rest ourselves, but the same privilege is to be extended to the children and to the servants; and even the strangers are to be included. If they are within our gates, they come under the ruling of the commandment. They are to be made acquainted with the custom of the household and the command of God, and invited to join in Sabbath observance. Out of courtesy and respect they will join, or else absent themselves so as to avoid any possible embarrassment. God wishes all in the home to have enough respect for the word of God to abstain from outward Sabbath profanation. The chief point, however, as we see it, is that God wants to make sure that no one comes to our home who is not made acquainted with His requirements and given an opportunity to join in our worship.

The Sabbath command includes even the cattle. To such as are not in the habit of being kind to animals, this may seem strange. God wants His people to be considerate of the brute creation. He notices the sufferings of all; not even a sparrow falls to the ground without His notice. Matt. 10:29. This shows innate kindness, and is a mighty commentary on the essential character of God. He is kind by nature. He is considerate, and He wants us to be the same.

As we review the Sabbath commandment, we notice that its chief demand is that of holiness. "Remember the Sabbath day, to *keep it holy.*" While cessation of labor is commanded, this is by no means all. He who abstains from work does not by that fact become a Sabbathkeeper and an heir of the promise. He may not do any work on God's day, but this is merely and at best a negative virtue. He is to keep the day *holy.* This means positive goodness. To the writer of Hebrews it means that man is to cease "from his own works, as God did from His." Heb. 4:10. The man who ceases from his own works, ceases from sin. Only such a man can keep the Sabbath as God wants it kept. Only he who is holy can keep the Sabbath holy.

This raises the Sabbath question from being merely the observance of a day to the living of a life. Out of the turmoil and struggle of the world, away from the battle for daily bread, God takes His people, gives them His Sabbath, and says: "Keep this day for Me. Cease from sin. Do righteousness. Meet with those of like faith for worship. Follow the example of your Master. Go about doing good. This day is a memorial of Eden, a memorial of creation. It is a foretaste of the Sabbath to come, a foretaste of heaven. It is My sign of sanctification. I have blessed the day. I will bless you and meet with you. Cease from your own works. Enter into My rest." Thus kept, the Sabbath becomes a blessed day indeed.

The First Sabbath

THE first sunset Adam ever saw was a Sabbath sunset. Thousands of years have passed since then, and tens of thousands of sunsets have testified to the fact that our God is a lover of glory and beauty. Men have again and again witnessed the miracle of night turning into day, and day into night, and have marveled at the exquisite beauty of the scene. They have, in the sunset, seen the wonder, the terror, the majesty, of Sinai; they have seen a replica of Golgotha as heavy clouds gathered about one space of clear, settled glory; they have seen the heavens bathed in the seraphic, wondrous beauty of Paradise as the color harmonies slowly changed from glory into glory, recording in the heavens a picture of unsurpassed loveliness and harmony, and in the soul a token of that peace which passes understanding. Yet with all this it is doubtful that there has ever been a sunset comparable to that first sunset, when God and man together witnessed the ushering in of the first Sabbath on earth.

God could have done many things in creation differently from the way He did, had His nature and purpose been merely utilitarian. When men want light or darkness, they turn a switch on or off, and the desired effect is immediately accomplished. God could have done the same. But He chose another way, the slower way, the way of beauty and wonder. Slowly He caused the light to fade, and the heavenly Artist shows what can be done with the dust of the earth, the mists of heaven, and the light from His appointed luminaries, as He mixes these ingredients in the laboratory of heaven and displays the result to man in the sunset. The God who causes a million flowers to bloom unseen, who places the pearl in the ocean and the amethyst among the rocks, must be a lover of beauty. Whatever God does, He accomplishes in the most exquisite and beautiful way. No wonder that man is asked to worship Him not only in holiness, but in the *beauty* of holiness.

Men have sinned and defaced the image of God. The earth itself is gradually being transformed, by the wickedness of men, from its original beauty into a shambles of horror and ugliness. But still "the heavens declare the glory of God; and the firmament showeth His handiwork. Day unto day uttereth speech, and night unto night showeth knowledge. There is no speech nor language, where their voice is not heard. Their line is gone out through all the earth, and their words to the end of the world. In them hath He set a tabernacle for the sun." Ps. 19:1-4.

Desolation may reign in the earth, death may stalk the highways, but God still speaks in and through nature, the heavens still declare the glory of God, and the sunsets still call men to worship the God of beauty, of peace, of love.

The Gift of the Sabbath

God had finished His work. Six days He had labored, and now evening was approaching, the evening that would usher in the Sabbath. God was not weary; yet "on the seventh day He rested, and was refreshed." Isa. 40:28; Ex. 31:17. He had finished creation, and had given to man everything that a loving Father could devise. As a crowning act He had given Adam a helpmeet, and in their new-found love Adam and Eve had walked through the garden, drinking in its beauty and rejoicing in their mutual love for their heavenly Father, who had provided so bountifully for them, but who, above all, had given them life, beauteous, glorious, abundant life.

Now evening was coming on, and God Himself was walking in the cool of the day, surveying His work and pronouncing it good. He had provided all that heart could wish; and yet there was one more thing He wanted to do, one more gift He wished to bestow. Wonderful as was the earth, surpassingly lovely as was the garden, there was still something more glorious, more wonderful, and God wanted to give them a foretaste of it. And so God decided to give them in the Sabbath a bit of heaven, a day upon which they might in a special way commune with Him, a day of fellowship and special blessing.

"The Sabbath was made for man." Mark 2:27. It was made differently, however, from the way in which other things were made. Of the rest of creation it is stated, "He spake, and it was done; He commanded, and it stood fast." By divine fiat the world and the things that are therein were called into existence. But not so with the Sabbath. God did not say, "Let there be a Sabbath," and there was a Sabbath. The Sabbath was not made in a minute, nor by divine fiat only. Three distinct acts of God are recorded as being requisite to the making of the Sabbath.

The First Step

"On the seventh day God ended His work which He had made; and He rested on the seventh day from all His work which He had made. And God blessed the seventh day, and sanctified it: because that in it He had rested from all His work which God created and made." Gen. 2:2, 3.

First, God rested. This rest was a matter of example, for, as already noted, God was not weary. Yet resting was a necessary part in the making of the Sabbath. As

God's rest was an example for man to follow, it was necessary that He rest as long as He expected man to rest; that
is, not merely part of the day, but the whole day. Hence
the statement is made that God rested not merely *on* or *in*
the seventh day, but that He "rested *the* seventh day."
Ex. 20:11.

If God rested the seventh day, how are we to understand
the statement that "on the seventh day God ended His
work which He had made"? Gen. 2:2, 3. Some have
thought that there must be a mistake in the record, as it
does not seem consistent to say that the heavens and the
earth were finished in six days, and yet that God ended
His work on the seventh day. Should not the record read
that God ended His work on the *sixth* day rather than
on the *seventh*? We think not. The statement that the
heavens and the earth were finished in six days is true; and
so is the statement that God ended His work on the
seventh day. The heavens and the earth were indeed
finished, but God's work was not ended. He had yet to
make the Sabbath, and this He could do only on the
Sabbath. And so God made the Sabbath on the Sabbath,
and He made it by resting. That *ended* His work. The
Sabbath was the finishing touch. Only when He had made
the Sabbath was His work done.

It is eminently fitting that God should end His work on
the seventh day, thus making the Sabbath a definite part
of creation, a part which cannot be detached or separated
from the rest. Had God ended His work on the sixth day,
some might think that the Sabbath was not part of God's
original plan, and that hence it might safely be ignored.
Whoever believes in a finished creation must of necessity
believe in the Sabbath; and conversely, whoever does not
believe in the Sabbath does not believe in a finished creation of God. To this the writer of Hebrews has reference
when he speaks of the seventh day, and notes that "the

works were finished from the foundation of the world." Heb. 4:3. God completed His work on the seventh day by making the Sabbath on that day. The record reads, "God blessed the seventh day, and sanctified it." Gen. 2:3.

There are those who think that it would be better if God had said that He blessed the *Sabbath* day instead of the *seventh* day. But the reading is doubtless as God wants it. Had it merely said that God blessed the Sabbath day, some might think that it referred to any day on which the Sabbath might come, and that if the first day of the week should be chosen as the Sabbath, the blessing would apply to that day. To forestall any such interpretation, God states that He blessed the seventh day, not the first, or the third, or any other day, but the seventh day. Hence the seventh day is a blessed day.

If some should protest that this interpretation confines the blessing to the seventh day, but does not call this day the Sabbath day, we would answer that God in the Sabbath commandment unites the seventh day and the Sabbath by stating that God "rested the *seventh* day: wherefore the Lord blessed the Sabbath day, and hallowed it." Ex. 20:11. Here the seventh day and the Sabbath are united, and the seventh day is identified as the Sabbath which God blessed. This seals and completes the evidence. God blessed the seventh day, and that day is the Sabbath.

God did not bless the Sabbath in *general,* nor did He bless *a* Sabbath, nor even *the* Sabbath, but the Sabbath *day,* and this Sabbath day is the *seventh* day. Doubtless these statements are so very precise and definite for a reason. God wanted no misunderstanding or dispute in regard to what He said or meant. He has done all that could be done to make the matter clear. He could not have been more specific.

When God blessed the Sabbath day, He had already blessed man. Gen. 1:28. This blessing included fruitfulness and the promise of dominion over the beasts of the field and over every living thing. As God blessed Abraham, that he might be a blessing, so He blessed Adam and Eve. They were to be fruitful and multiply, and be a blessing to their offspring as well as to the beasts of the field, over which they were to bear gentle rule.

The Second Step

We can understand how God can bless human beings. We can even understand how He can bless animals and give them their work to do in carrying out God's purpose; but how can God bless a *day,* a division of time, neither animate nor inanimate, not alive nor dead, a thing without substance, a conception rather than a reality; time, which defies definition, though all mankind is aware of its existence and reality? How can time be blessed so as to be a blessing to man?

The answer is that time does not have any virtue or power in itself to be a blessing or a help to others. Time is as impersonal as space, and equally inconceivable. One difference between the two is noticeable: space extends in all directions, while time might be compared to a one-way road, permitting traffic in one direction only. Man has no power over time, to hasten or retard it. Whether he will or not, he is carried along with it, and despite all protests is one day older tomorrow than he is today. He cannot reverse the process, however much he may wish to do so. Time is superior to him, and he obeys its mandates.

There are those who believe that God did not create time, but that in some way He found it already existing. But this cannot be. Time and space are not self-existent entities, operating apart from God and independent of Him. If that were true, they would be equal with God, or even His superior; for that which is coeval with God or exists prior to God must at least be equal with

Him; and that which is not created by God is self-existent and is God. The Christian believes that "without Him was not anything made that was made," and that time and space are created by God as verily as anything else He has made. John 1:3.

Though the two conceptions of time and space are beyond human comprehension, each is helpful in understanding the other. Our conception of space, for example, helps us to understand time better, and how it is possible for God to bless time.

We go to church to worship God, and enter the edifice dedicated to Him. The church building is merely four walls enclosing a part of space. The space within the walls does not appear to be different from the space outside. And yet there is a difference. Something has happened to it. It is holy space, space dedicated to the service of God. God is present in the building in a sense in which He is not present outside the building. God has divided space from space—one is holy; the other is not. Explain it we cannot. But we may believe that it is so.

As God can set aside space where He chooses to reveal Himself, so God can set aside time. Out of the vast ocean of time—as out of space—He chooses a portion, blesses it, and turns it over as blessed time for man to use. It appears to be the same kind of time as other time, and yet it is different. It is blessed time, and is not to be used for common purposes which in themselves might be lawful. As we would not use a dedicated cathedral for business purposes—perfectly lawful in themselves—so we are not to use God's holy time for common pursuits, however legitimate they might be in themselves. When God's people meet in the appointed place on the Sabbath to worship, they are thrice blessed: they themselves are a blessed people; the place in which they worship is blessed; the very time of worship is blessed. A holy people worships a holy

47

God at a holy time in a holy place. Surely, under such conditions God's richest blessing may be expected.

The Third Step

"God blessed the seventh day, and sanctified it." The sanctification of the seventh day is the third step in the making of the Sabbath, which we shall now consider.

Genesis 2:3 states that God "blessed the seventh day, and sanctified it: because that in it He had rested from all His works which God created and made." We notice first that the reason given for God's blessing and sanctifying the seventh day is *"because* that in it He had rested." Man is not here mentioned. Man had not worked; he had been brought into existence on the sixth day, and had had no opportunity to work. But God had worked. He had worked six days, and had rested the seventh. Having finished both His labor and His rest, He blessed and sanctified the Sabbath. The reading is that God blessed the day "because that in it He had rested."

There can be no reason for God's blessing a day for His own use. His blessing and sanctification must of necessity be for someone else's sake. God is holy; He is always holy; He is no more holy at one time than at another. His holiness does not admit of degrees. But this is not so with men and places. They are holy in proportion to their nearness to God.

It was to impress this upon the people that a curtain was stretched about the sanctuary of old, enclosing the court. As man was approaching the God of holiness, there was a gradual elimination of the common and the profane. In the first court all worshipers were permitted, Israelites and strangers. In the second court only Israelites could come—they were God's chosen people. In the next court only Levites and priests were permitted, such as had work to do about the tabernacle. Inside the sanctuary itself, in the first apartment, only priests could officiate, such as had been chosen by lot for this work. The priests could not enter the sanctuary merely because they were priests. That, as has been noted, was reserved for only a chosen few. And these could not enter the second apartment, the most holy. That was reserved for one man only, the high priest; and even he could enter it only at specified times, and after long physical and spiritual preparation. God is most holy, and could be approached only after prolonged heart preparation and deep humiliation of soul.

All this was to teach man God's holiness. Wherever God reveals Himself, the place becomes holy, whether it be a burning bush in the wilderness or the most holy place in the sanctuary. Also, if God removes His presence, as He did when the veil was rent in Herod's temple, the place immediately becomes common. It is God's presence that makes a thing or a place or a person holy. This has a definite bearing on the Sabbath. God sanctified it. He made it holy. And it was made holy by His presence.

To sanctify, according to Webster, means "to make sacred or holy; to set apart to a sacred office or to religious use; . . . to hallow." As it is impossible to impart moral qualities to insensate things, sanctification, as applied to the seventh day, must mean the same as sanctification in the case of the tabernacle and its furniture. Moses was commanded concerning the altar, "Seven days thou shalt make an atonement for the altar, and sanctify it; and it shall be an altar most holy: whatsoever toucheth the altar shall be holy." Ex. 29:37. In like manner the whole sanctuary, the ark, the vessels, the candlestick, and all that pertained thereto, was sanctified, and could henceforth be used only in the sacred service of the sanctuary ritual. Ex. 30:26-29.

As a religious edifice is dedicated and set apart for

4

religious purposes, so the Sabbath was dedicated, sanctified, and set apart for holy use. The sanctification, of course, had reference to the future, and not to the past. The dedication of a church edifice takes place at a definite time, but its effect is pointed toward the future. As the ordination of a minister to the sacred work of God is a definite act looking to his future usefulness in God's cause, so the sanctification of the Sabbath was a forward-looking act, having the good of mankind in view.

We emphasize this matter, which indeed is self-evident, for a reason that there are those who insist that the blessing and sanctification of the seventh day had reference to the original Sabbath, and to that Sabbath only, and not to succeeding ones. Such a statement seems altogether unwarranted, and even absurd. As well claim that the dedication of a church, the sanctification of holy utensils, the setting apart of a man to the holy work of the ministry, are acts that refer to that particular moment only, and immediately thereafter become of none effect.

The Sabbath Made for Man

"The Sabbath was made for man." Mark 2:27. It was not made for God or for the angels, good or bad; it was not made for the lower creatures or for nature; it was not made for any particular class or race, not made for Jew or Gentile; it was made for man, mankind, the whole human race. As a kind, thoughtful parent presents a gift to his child for its use and enjoyment, so God made the Sabbath for man. Adam and Eve constituted the whole of mankind in the beginning; hence the Sabbath was made for them, for their children, and for their children's children. Only in this way could the Sabbath be said to be made for man.

If it was the original creation Sabbath only that was blessed and sanctified, we see little point to the statement that the Sabbath was made for man; nor do we see how it in any way could be a blessing to man. It would merely be a historical occurrence, a constantly receding point in time, ever growing smaller, a point to which man would be unable ever to return, an incident that had little meaning or importance as far as any present blessing to mankind is concerned.

One time Christ and the disciples were walking through the fields on the Sabbath day. The disciples were hungry and plucked some of the corn, an act which was considered lawful on other days, but which the Pharisees did not permit on the Sabbath. Always on the alert to find some cause for complaint against Christ, the Pharisees immediately went to Him, saying, "Behold, why do they on the Sabbath day that which is not lawful?" Mark 2:24.

Christ was not slow in defending what they had done. He told the Pharisees that the Sabbath was intended to be a blessing to mankind, not a burden or a yoke. It was lawful to do well on the Sabbath; it was lawful to minister to the needs of mankind; and, citing David, He tells them that it was lawful to do what the disciples had done. Then He announces the true principle of Sabbathkeeping: "The Sabbath was made for man, and not man for the Sabbath." To this He adds the significant words, "Therefore the Son of man is Lord also of the Sabbath." Mark 2:27, 28.

We believe that Christ had a particular reason for declaring Himself Lord of the Sabbath. This we discuss in another place, and shall not dwell on it here. We would like, however, to call attention to the fact that Christ considered the Sabbath a vital factor in religion, directed its proper observance, and proclaimed Himself Lord of it. This does not give the impression that Christ believed the Sabbath to be merely of historical importance. He considered it a living reality, an institution to be defended from Pharisaical intrusion, an institution of which He was Lord.

The Hebrew word for "sanctify" is generally so translated throughout the Old Testament. There are a few exceptions, however. To two of these we call attention as we close this study.

When the cities of refuge were selected as places to which a manslayer might flee to escape the wrath of the avenger of blood, "they appointed Kedesh in Galilee." Joshua 20:7. The word here translated "appointed" is the same word that is elsewhere used for "sanctify," as the marginal reading confirms.

The other translation of the word is found in 2 Kings 10:20, where "proclaim" is found. "Jehu said, Proclaim a solemn assembly for Baal."

From these Biblical uses of the word we are warranted in affirming that when God sanctified the seventh day, He set it apart for a holy use, He appointed it as the Sabbath, He proclaimed it a holy day. As Lord of the Sabbath Christ announces that He made it for man, to be a blessing and a help to him, to serve as a reminder of creation and His love to man. It is His special gift to mankind, who need it even more than the holy pair in the garden.

The Sabbath at Sinai

GENESIS, the first book of the Bible, is a condensed account that covers the first twenty-five hundred years of earth's history, nearly one half of all recorded time. It embraces such epoch-making subjects as creation, Paradise, Adam and Eve, Satan, the fall, the flood, Noah, Abraham, Isaac, Jacob, Joseph, the seven-year famine, and the descent of Israel into Egypt. Genesis is not a book of law, or a compendium of theology, or a scientific treatise, but a simple record of what took place in the early history of the race.

Opponents of the Sabbath point with apparent satisfaction to the fact that the Sabbath is not mentioned in Genesis after its first institution by God. If the Sabbath is as important as its advocates seem to think, they reason, it should have been given a prominent place in the account of those centuries.

This reasoning, however, is neither sound nor safe. We noted above that Genesis is not a book of law or a code of ethics. It has another purpose entirely. There is in it no Sabbath commandment, but neither is any of the other commandments found there. Genesis is not a book of commands, as is the following book, Exodus. On this line of reasoning Cain could have successfully challenged God to show him the commandment that says, "Thou shalt not kill." There is no such commandment recorded in Genesis; but it would be precarious on this ground to argue its

53

nonexistence. It would be as reasonable to contend that as there is no record that God ever forbade Adam and Eve to worship other gods, they were at liberty to make images and bow down to them; or, seeing there is no recorded commandment in Genesis that forbids adultery, that Joseph would not have sinned had he yielded to the temptress. Genesis is a condensed account of a long period of time, and it cannot be expected that it should contain all that modern scholars demand. It should be noted, however, that the Sabbath holds a very prominent place in this book. Genesis records the institution and observance of the Sabbath by the Creator Himself. In this it holds the preeminence over all the other commandments. It could hardly have been given more prominence.

Moses and Aaron

The book of Exodus opens with the account of Israel in hard bondage in Egypt. When they first went down to Egypt, Israel had been favored by the king. But soon a new king arose, who did not know Joseph, and when the children of Israel multiplied to the point where they threatened to become a potential political problem, they were put under restriction and hard bondage. In their trouble they called upon the Lord, and Moses was sent to deliver them.

As a babe Moses had been rescued by the daughter of Pharaoh, and had been brought up at the royal court. Here he became learned in all the wisdom of the Egyptians, but withal remained true to the faith of his fathers. When on a certain occasion he saw injustice done to one of the Israelites, he promptly killed the Egyptian at fault. Because of this he was compelled to flee from Egypt, and spent forty years in the wilderness herding sheep.

It was in the wilderness that the call came to him to go back to Egypt and deliver the people. He felt himself unprepared for the task, but God gave him a helper in Aaron, his brother. Together they proceeded to Pharaoh, demanding that he let Israel go. Pharaoh was astonished at their audacity, and demanded, "Who is the Lord, that I should obey His voice to let Israel go? I know not the Lord, neither will I let Israel go." Ex. 5:2.

During their sojourn in Egypt Israel had neglected the ordinances of the Lord, and His worship had fallen in decay. Moses and Aaron were concerned about this, and prayed Pharaoh, "Thus saith the Lord, . . . Let My people go, that they may hold a feast unto Me in the wilderness. . . . Let us go, we pray thee, three days' journey into the desert, and sacrifice unto the Lord our God." Verses 1-3.

This was before the law was given on Sinai, and before any feasts had been appointed by God to be observed as part of the ceremonial sanctuary service. The Passover had not been instituted, nor any other sacred festival, with the exception of the seventh-day Sabbath. We are not informed which festival Moses had in mind when he demanded that the people be given permission to go three days into the desert to "hold a feast . . . in the wilderness, . . . and sacrifice unto the Lord our God." Was it the seventh-day Sabbath which Israel had neglected, and which Moses was attempting to restore? We are not told, but there are certain significant allusions which make this not only possible, but probable.

Pharaoh's complaint to Moses, "Ye make them rest from their burdens," may be considered a correct translation, but it does not give the peculiar phrasing of the Hebrew, which might better be translated, "Ye cause them to Sabbatize." The Hebrew word used is *shabbathon,* a definite allusion to the Sabbath. The writer of Exodus could have used another word for resting had he so desired, a word that would not have raised the question of

Sabbathkeeping. That he chose this particular word is significant.

At the time when Israel was in Egypt, the only Sabbath in existence was the seventh-day Sabbath, instituted at creation. No other feast, not even the Passover, had come into being. When Pharaoh, therefore, complains that Moses and Aaron made the people "Sabbatize," the preponderence of evidence favors the weekly Sabbath. In line with this is the other complaint that "Moses and Aaron let the people from their works." "Let" means to hinder, to cause to cease. This indicates that Pharaoh held Moses and Aaron responsible for the people's not working; that is, for the people's "Sabbatizing." "Ye are idle, ye are idle," said Pharaoh; "therefore ye say, Let us go and do sacrifice to the Lord." Ex. 5:17. While we would not contend that the evidence here presented is final, we believe that the fact that no other Sabbaths or feasts were in existence at this time, favors the view that it was the seventh-day Sabbath that was in question.

The Sabbath Before Sinai

Though Pharaoh at first declined to let Israel go, he consented to do so as the plagues became increasingly more severe. With a mighty hand and a stretched-out arm God delivered His people from Egypt and brought them into the wilderness. In honor of their deliverance, they sang the song of glorious victory recorded in the fifteenth chapter of Exodus. It was only through the mercy of God that they had been saved from Pharaoh's pursuing army. To Him they gave the praise.

Having brought them out of Egypt, God now told them upon what conditions they might expect His continued protection. Said God: "If thou wilt diligently hearken to the voice of the Lord thy God, and wilt do that which is right in His sight, and wilt give ear to His commandments, and keep all His statutes, I will put none of these diseases upon thee, which I have brought upon the Egyptians: for I am the Lord that healeth thee." Ex. 15:26. This is a most beautiful promise given to them on the condition that they "give ear to His commandments, and keep all His statutes."

The bread which the people had brought with them from Egypt did not last many days, and they soon became hungry and began to murmur. "Would to God," they said, "that we had died by the hand of the Lord in the land of Egypt, when we sat by the fleshpots, and when we did eat bread to the full; for ye have brought us forth into this wilderness, to kill this whole assembly with hunger." Ex. 16:3. The Lord quickly answered them, "I will rain bread from heaven for you; and the people shall go out and gather a certain rate every day, *that I may prove them, whether they will walk in My law, or no.*" Verse 4.

This was before the law had been proclaimed from Sinai. God was about to make Israel His peculiar people, but before He did so He wished to "prove them, whether they will walk in My law, or no."

Moses now called the people together and instructed them. "This is that which the Lord hath said, Tomorrow is the rest of the holy Sabbath unto the Lord: bake that which ye will bake today, and seethe that ye will seethe; and that which remaineth over lay up for you to be kept until the morning." Verse 23. This instruction concerned the preparation for the Sabbath. On the sixth day they were to do their baking and cooking, both for that day and for the Sabbath. They were each day to gather manna for one day, but on the sixth day they were to gather a double portion, for Moses had announced to them that no manna would fall on the Sabbath. Friday they were to do all their cooking, and on the Sabbath they were to eat that which they had prepared.

On the Sabbath Moses said to them, "Eat that today; for today is a Sabbath unto the Lord: today ye shall not find it in the field. Six days ye shall gather it; but on the seventh day, which is the Sabbath, in it there shall be none."

Despite all that God had said, "there went out some of the people on the seventh day for to gather." Verse 27. They had had definite instruction. There could be no misunderstanding. They knew just what they should do and what was expected of them; yet they "went out . . . on the seventh day for to gather." "And the Lord said unto Moses, How long refuse ye to keep My commandments and My laws? See, for that the Lord hath given you the Sabbath, therefore He giveth you on the sixth day the bread of the two days; abide ye every man in his place, let no man go out of his place on the seventh day. So the people rested on the seventh day." Verses 28-30.

This account is illuminating. The people had just come out of Egypt, and many of the Egyptian customs and traditions were still clinging to them. At the least provocation they were ready to murmur against God and turn to their idols. They were far from being what God desired His people to be. Before He could accept them and make of them a great nation, He must teach them His statutes and test them, that He might know whether they would walk in His law or no.

The Sabbath Not a New Institution

The Sabbath is not here presented as a new institution that is now being introduced for the first time. Rather, it appears to be well known. Nor is the law new to them. God speaks familiarly to them of the law, and promises them freedom from sickness if they will "give ear to His commandments, and keep all His statutes." Ex. 15:26. This phraseology is practically the same as that used of

Abraham many years previously, "Abraham obeyed My voice, and kept My charge, My commandments, My statutes, and My laws." Gen. 26:5.

From this we know that God's commandments, statutes, and laws were known to Abraham, that he kept them, and that he taught his children to keep them. Gen. 18:19. Isaac and Jacob were his son and his grandson, being respectively seventy-five and fifteen years old at the death of Abraham. It was Jacob who later went to Egypt. We are therefore assured that the children of Israel in Egypt knew of God's law and His statutes, and that when God spoke to them familiarly of keeping His commandments, they knew exactly what He meant.

Those who hold that the law of God and the Sabbath were not known before Moses and Sinai are not well informed. Abraham knew of God's commandments, statutes, and laws, and he taught his children after him. God Himself observed the seventh-day Sabbath in the Garden of Eden; so Adam and Eve were acquainted with the Sabbath. Of Cain and Abel it is stated that "at the end of days" they went up to worship before the Lord, bringing their offering. Gen. 4:3, margin.

The phrase, "at the end of days," which is the correct Hebrew rendering, is an interesting one, and naturally raises the question, The end of which days? There can be an "end of days" only as a series of days is involved, having a beginning and an end.

When God worked six days and rested the seventh, when He told man to work the next six days and rest the seventh, He measured off a week of seven days, and the end of the week saw "the end of days." Without the Sabbath there would be no division point; but when the Sabbath was instituted, there was made an "end of days," and when men came to seven, they would begin counting over again. God Himself made this division.

When Cain and Abel, therefore, came to bring their offerings to God "at the end of days," they came to worship on the Sabbath. It may be presumed that Abel desired to worship, for he was a follower of God; but the same cannot be said of Cain. Yet he worshiped also, and at the same time that Abel worshiped. This leads us to believe that there was a stated time for worship, and that it was not merely a coincidence that they happened to come there at the same time. In any event they went up to worship together, and this was "at the end of days." Commentators are generally agreed that this can refer to nothing but the Sabbath. We believe they are right.

Adam and Eve had God's example of Sabbathkeeping. Cain and Abel worshiped "at the end of days." Abraham knew of God's commandments, statutes, and laws, kept them, and taught his children to keep them. And now God decided to prove whether Israel would keep His law, or no.

Israel was in the wilderness, where there was no opportunity to till the land or have large flocks of cattle as they had had in Egypt. Unless food was provided for them in some supernatural way, they would starve. God therefore proposed to feed them with bread from heaven, while at the same time He gave them an object lesson in Sabbathkeeping.

God caused the manna to fall six days of each week. There is no reason why God could not have let manna rain down from heaven every other day, had He so desired, or every third day, or one day a week only, or seven days a week. But God chose to let the manna fall six days, and to let none fall on the seventh day. To make up for this loss, He let twice as much fall on the sixth day as fell on the other days, so that there would be sufficient for all needs on the seventh day. This would be an effective way to teach Israel two important things: to work six days and to rest on the seventh.

But God did more than this. He so arranged matters that the manna would keep only one day, and after that it would spoil. That made it doubly necessary for the people to gather every day; that is, to work six days. God could just as well have arranged it so that the manna would keep two days, or seven, or any other number of days. When He made it keep only one day, He did it for a purpose, as already noted.

But what about the Sabbath, when no manna fell? That in itself would make the Sabbath stand out above the other days. Could He do anything else to impress upon the minds of the people the sacredness of the Sabbath? Yes, if God should miraculously preserve the manna from spoiling on the Sabbath, that would be an added lesson to them in Sabbathkeeping. And so God decided to have the manna keep only one day during the week, but on the Sabbath He kept it so that it did not breed worms. The first was a lesson in working six days; the second, a lesson in keeping holy the Sabbath.

The falling of the manna thus had another and a greater purpose than merely feeding the people. That could have been done in other ways. It was rather a national lesson in Sabbathkeeping as related to the seventh day. Had this lesson been given once, it would have been of tremendous significance in regard to God's estimate of the Sabbath. Had it been repeated twice, there could have been no doubt regarding God's intent. Had it been repeated week after week for a year, all would know that God wanted to impress the lesson of the Sabbath upon Israel so deeply and thoroughly that they would never forget it. What shall we say, then, when this lesson was repeated not once or twice or ten times, but more than two thousand times; that is, fifty-two times a year for forty years! If Israel had not learned the lesson by that time, there could be no reason for continuing the lesson.

That the lesson of the manna might ever be kept in mind, God commanded that a pot of manna be placed in the ark where the ten commandments were kept, to be a perpetual reminder of the Sabbath as well as of God's sustaining power, Ex. 16:32-36. This manna did not spoil. It was to be kept for "generations." It was a reminder of God's care and pointed directly to the Sabbath commandment. The real intent of the miracle of the manna was not the feeding of the people. That was only incidental. God's chief purpose was to teach Israel Sabbathkeeping. He was proving them. He was preparing them to enter into covenant relation with Him.

The Sabbath at Sinai

In the third month after Israel departed out of Egypt, they came into the Wilderness of Sinai. Never had a people seen the power of God manifested in such a striking way as had Israel during those two months. Now they were to witness the climax. God had marvelously helped them in Egypt. While thousands of the Egyptians had been stricken down at their side in the plagues, and ten thousand at their right hand, the plagues had not come nigh them. Wonderful had been their deliverance at the Red Sea from the pursuing armies of Pharaoh, and still more wonderful their deliverance from hunger by having bread rain down from heaven. When they were thirsty, God made sweet the bitter water at Marah; and when Amalek attacked them, God discomfited the enemy, and Israel won a glorious victory. They had lacked nothing, and their experience would lead them to believe that whatever the future might hold for them, they would be safe if they only followed the Lord. God had told them the conditions upon which they might expect His help; He had admonished them to "give ear to His commandments, and keep all His statutes," and He promised that if they did so,

He would lead and protect them. In particular had He called their attention to the Sabbath; and to help them keep this ever in mind, He had weekly, before their very eyes, performed miracles, so that only the most willful would dare transgress the holy commandment.

By this time Israel understood well what was required of them. The question that remained was Israel's willingness to abide by the conditions laid down for God's continued presence and blessing. God intended to make them His own people. He would continue to work mightily for them if they were willing to co-operate with Him. But He would not forcibly compel them to do His will. He had a work to do in the earth, and He invited Israel to share with Him the task of filling the earth with the knowledge and glory of God.

In pursuance of this object God called Moses to Him in the mount and asked him to communicate to Israel His desire. "Thus shalt thou say to the house of Jacob, and tell the children of Israel: Ye have seen what I did unto the Egyptians, and how I bare you on eagles' wings, and brought you unto Myself. Now therefore, if ye will obey My voice indeed, and keep My covenant, then ye shall be a peculiar treasure unto Me above all people: for all the earth is Mine: and ye shall be unto Me a kingdom of priests, and a holy nation. These are the words which thou shalt speak unto the children of Israel." Ex. 19:3-6.

Accordingly Moses called the elders of the people "and laid before their faces all these words which the Lord commanded him. And all the people answered together, and said, All that the Lord hath spoken we will do. And Moses returned the words of the people unto the Lord. And the Lord said unto Moses, Lo, I come unto thee in a thick cloud, that the people may hear when I speak with thee, and believe thee forever. And Moses told the words of the people unto the Lord." Ex. 19:7-9.

God now asked Moses to get the people ready to enter into covenant with Him, "for the third day the Lord will come down in the sight of all the people upon Mt. Sinai." Moses communicated the words of God to the people, and on the third day all assembled before the mount to hear the conditions of the covenant announced.

It is to be remembered that Israel had already witnessed the mighty power of the Lord in various ways. But despite all this they did not have a full understanding of the holiness and majesty of God, or of their relation to Him. True, God had helped them defeat Amalek, He had destroyed Pharaoh and his army, and He had smitten the Egyptians with the plagues. And He had protected His own. The plagues had not come nigh them; they had murmured when there was no water, but no punishment had come because of their murmuring. When they had complained about the lack of food, God had provided them with manna; and again there had been no rebuke. They might easily come to the conclusion that while other peoples would be punished, Israel would not; other people might get sick, but not they. They were the Lord's own; they could do as they pleased, and nothing would ever harm them.

Israel had misunderstood the goodness of the Lord, and it was necessary to set them right. While they were or would be the people of God, it was only on condition of obedience. They needed to learn that if they disobeyed, they would be no better off than other nations which the Lord had destroyed because of their wickedness. God must give Israel a demonstration of His holiness, a demonstration they would never forget. They had seen what God did to other nations. They must now be shown that God is no respecter of persons; they must be impressed with the majesty of the law which they were about to hear proclaimed; and the demonstration must be such that they would get a wholesome fear of ever transgressing the commandments of God. They needed just such a lesson.

At the appointed time Israel was gathered about the mount, which was fenced off, so that neither man nor animal might unwittingly trespass on holy ground. "Sinai was altogether on a smoke, because the Lord descended upon it in fire: and the smoke thereof ascended as the smoke of a furnace, and the whole mount quaked greatly. And when the voice of the trumpet sounded long, and waxed louder and louder, Moses spake, and God answered him by a voice." Verses 18, 19.

God then came down upon Mt. Sinai and spoke to them the ten commandments, as recorded in Exodus 20. Even Moses was not unaffected by the display of glory. The writer of Hebrews remarks that "so terrible was the sight that Moses said, I exceedingly fear and quake." Heb. 12:21.

The demonstration of sternness and power which God gave on Mt. Sinai is not His ordinary way of working. God is not usually stern, nor does He make a show of His power. Rather, He delights in doing His work quietly, unnoticed almost, as is evident in the mighty but silent forces of the universe. But there are times when a demonstration is needed. Certain people and certain circumstances demand it. As there are children and grown persons whose respect is gained only by a demonstration of physical force, so there are nations and peoples who will learn no other way. And Israel needed this lesson. And so God gave it to them. The same lesson is needed by many today.

God would gladly guide His people with His eye. A hint regarding God's will should be enough—and is enough —for the informed and willing Christian. God does not like to use bridle and bit, but at times they are necessary. God would much rather speak with the small, still voice;

5

He would much rather whisper to us than thunder at us. But in any event He wants us to learn the lesson. "See that ye refuse not Him that speaketh. For if they escaped not who refused Him that spake on earth, much more shall not we escape, if we turn away from Him that speaketh from heaven: whose voice then shook the earth: but now He hath promised, saying, Yet once more I shake not the earth only, but also heaven." Heb. 12:25, 26.

The Sabbath Commandment

In the law proclaimed on Sinai, the Sabbath commandment looms large. Before this God had given Israel a visual demonstration of His high regard for the Sabbath. In fact, the very week the commandment was announced from Mt. Sinai, the manna fell copiously on the sixth day, and on the Sabbath none fell, a reminder of God's desire in regard to the day of rest. Of all the commandments, this was the one that was emphasized; for the Sabbath was the day in which Israel would have time to instruct their children in the ways of God. If this day were disregarded, all the commandments would be neglected. The keeping of this commandment would affect the keeping of all the others. It was the one and only commandment that provided time for the contemplation of God and His works.

There is nothing in the proclamation of the law on Sinai that would make one feel that the keeping of the commandments, or any one of them, is an optional matter. The world has never witnessed such a demonstration as was there given, and never will witness another like it till men shall see the Son of man coming in the clouds of heaven. God Himself could not make more emphatic that inclusion in the covenant and the favor of God were dependent upon the faithful performance of the terms announced.

A question now arises that deserves consideration: Is the

ten-commandment law meant to apply to the whole world, or is it applicable to Israel only, and of no concern to Christians? This is an important question. There is little dispute about the nine commandments; so the question really concerns the fourth only. Are Christians to keep the fourth commandment?

While this question will be discussed more fully as we consider the New Testament aspects of the Sabbath, it may be well at this time to make some general observations on the law.

The ten commandments have all the earmarks of a universal law. In fact, we doubt that the question of its universality would ever be raised were it not for the fourth commandment. All agree that the commandments that deal with stealing, swearing, killing, coveting, and worshiping God are applicable not to a few only, but to all classes and nations of men. Their universal application is admitted, and we would feel under no obligation to convince a man who thought otherwise. We consider that point settled. We therefore come back to the question of the Sabbath commandment. Does this commandment belong to the moral law?

We would not know how to account for the existence of a nonmoral commandment in the midst of the moral law. This would seem to call for an explanation on the part of those who hold such a view. The preponderance of evidence is in favor of the Sabbath commandment's being of the same nature as the other commandments. The burden of proof rests upon those who think differently.

However, we do not wish to dispose of the matter in this negative fashion. We believe that the Sabbath commandment is a moral commandment on a level with the others; in fact, it underlies them all. It would be easier to dispose of some of the other commandments than to dispose of the Sabbath commandment.

The first three commandments deal with God and His worship. We are to have no other gods before Him. We are not to make any image or any likeness of anything in heaven and earth, and worship it. We are to be reverent and respectful and not take the name of the Lord in vain. Then comes the Sabbath commandment which defines the time of rest when we are to worship and attend to the things of the spirit. Had this commandment been left out, there would have been no stated time commanded in which to worship. In that case it would have been necessary for men to come to some agreement among themselves in regard to the best time when this might be done. That is, had God not appointed a day, men would of necessity have had to supply the omission, for without such a day there could be no corporate worship. If God is to be worshiped by His people; if there is to be any united adoration of the most high God; if there is to be any order and system in religion, time must definitely be planned for and given to it. This makes the Sabbath a necessity. Its omission from the decalogue would be fatal to religion. Let us repeat, If God had not appointed a day, men would have had to do so. A day of worship belongs to religion.

We have noted above and wish to emphasize it, that the Sabbath underlies all the commandments, providing as it does the time needed for the contemplation of man's duty to his Maker and his fellow men. God considered this of so much importance that He deigned to give the example for man to follow. In view of this, how can anyone think that the Sabbath commandment does not belong to the moral law? If there were no other reason than the fact that God has commanded the Sabbath day to be kept holy, this would be reason enough to put it on a moral basis. But when we consider the plan of God with regard to the Sabbath, that it is this day upon which He depends for the instruction of His children in the ways of God; that this is the time which He Himself has set apart for this most important work; and that without this time jealously guarded, God would be deprived of the worship due Him— when we take all this into consideration, we are clear that not only does the Sabbath have a place in the moral law, not only is it a moral commandment in itself, but that in a certain sense it is that which binds all the commandments together, that which binds earth and heaven together, provides unity among the people of God, and places the spiritual stamp upon all. Let no one despise or reject the Sabbath of God. Let no one neglect it. In the keeping of it there is great blessing.

The Sabbath in the Old Testament

SOME have objected to the Sabbath as being a Jewish institution. They maintain that the Sabbath was given to the Jews, and that hence it is not for the Christians. We admit that it was given to the Jews on Mt. Sinai. But so was the commandment, "Thou shalt not steal." The one is as much Jewish as the other. In fact, all the commandments were given to the Jews. The Jews were told not to kill, commit adultery, swear falsely, or covet. All these commandments are Jewish, if the Sabbath is Jewish. Christ also was given to the Jews; He was born of a Jewish mother and was reared in a Jewish home. The prophets were all Jews, the apostles were all Jews, the gospel was first preached to the Jews, every one of the books of the New Testament was written by a Jew. Even when we get to heaven, we shall see the names of the twelve disciples of Christ, Jews, on the foundation stones of the New Jerusalem; on the gates of the city will be the names of twelve other Jews, the twelve sons of Israel. Abraham, Isaac, and Jacob, all Jews, will be prominent in the kingdom, and Christ will sit upon the throne of His father David, a Jew. Under these circumstances it is better for Christians not to speak sneeringly of the Sabbath of the Lord as being Jewish, as though that were a term of reproach. "He is not a Jew, which is one outwardly; neither is that circumcision, which is outward in the flesh: but he is a Jew, which is one inwardly." Rom. 2:28, 29.

71

It might be remarked, however, that the Sabbath is less "Jewish," if that were possible, than some of the other commandments; for the Sabbath shares the honor with marriage of stemming from Eden, before there were any Jews or Gentiles in existence. Marriage was regiven to the Jews, as was the Sabbath, but they are both the possession of mankind, not of any particular race or color.

"The Sabbath was made for man." These words are ever appropriate when the universality of the Sabbath is under consideration. They should forever settle the question of the Sabbath's being a Jewish institution. Christ made the Sabbath. He says that He made it for man. He knows. Jews are men, and so the Sabbath was made for them. Christians are men; so the Sabbath was made for them. Whoever claims the title and right to the name "man," may know that God made the Sabbath for him. The Sabbath is no more Jewish than are the other commandments.

Stoning for Sabbathbreaking

Each nation has its own peculiar way of dealing with offenders against its laws. Under certain conditions a nation may feel that horse stealing deserves capital punishment—as was the case in the newer section of the United States some years ago. Israel may erect cities of refuge as asylums to which a manslayer may flee under certain conditions and be safe until he has stood trial. Sexual crime may become rampant to the degree that capital punishment may be meted out for transgression. Israel may exact the death penalty for the violation of the Sabbath under certain peculiarly aggravating conditions; but this is not part of the commandment and does not affect the law itself. The Jews under theocratic rule had rules not of universal application or obligation. No one should confuse local regulations with universal principles.

Was there not a regulation among the Israelites in the wilderness that whoever transgressed the Sabbath willfully and "with a high hand" should be stoned? To this a qualified affirmative answer should be given; for it was not only to the Sabbath that this law applied, but to the transgression of any of the other commandments. The general law is found in Numbers 15:30, 31, and reads, "The soul that doeth aught presumptuously, whether he be born in the land, or a stranger, the same reproacheth the Lord; and that soul shall be cut off from among his people. Because he hath despised the word of the Lord, and hath broken His commandment, that soul shall utterly be cut off; his iniquity shall be upon him."

"Presumptuously" means, as the margin reads, with a "high hand," that is, knowingly, obstinately, defiantly. This law applied to all the commandments. Whenever a man transgressed presumptuously, there was only one penalty, death. Hence we read in Exodus 21:14 ff., that if a man killed another "presumptuously," they were to "take him from Mine altar, that he may die." Again, if a man smite his father or curse him, he "shall surely be put to death." If a man "stealeth a man, and selleth him," he "shall surely be put to death." These punishments were all for sins done "with a high hand," and applied to all the commandments alike.

The question whether this ruling applied to the Sabbath commandment arose early in Israel's history. To commit murder was always considered a serious offense. Was it as serious to transgress the Sabbath, or would such a transgression be winked at?

The issue arose when a man went out on the Sabbath to gather sticks. For some time manna had rained down from heaven. Israel had gathered their portion each day, but had been warned not to go out on the seventh day. At first, nevertheless, some had gone out on the Sabbath, but no special punishment had been meted out for their transgression.

Now, however, a long time had gone by. All knew God's requirements. Ignorance could no longer be pleaded as an excuse. Whoever should now profane the Sabbath would know what he was doing. His act would be one of defiance, and his punishment would not be primarily for his transgression, but for his defiance. The law had been announced from Sinai; God had also announced that any who presumptuously transgressed any of the commandments would be cut off. "He hath despised the word of the Lord, and hath broken His commandment, that soul shall utterly be cut off." Num. 15:31. Should any man transgress the Sabbath, he would despise "the word of the Lord," and in that act would challenge and defy God.

It was under these conditions that the man violated the Sabbath. He knew the law and what God had said. Despite this he went out. What now should be done? Did the Sabbath rank with the other commandments, or should a difference be made? Surely it was worse to kill a man than to gather sticks on the Sabbath.

However, as already noted, it was not the thing done that alone counted; it was rather the attitude. It was not for gathering up sticks that he was punished; it was *"because he hath despised the word of the Lord."* His gathering sticks was only a means of showing his contempt for God.

Moses, however, wanted to make doubly sure of what he should do in this particular case. He therefore put the man in confinement until God should make His will known. On this decision much would hang, for it would now be known for a certainty whether the Sabbath commandment should take its place with the other commandments and its transgression be counted equally serious. God Himself gave the decision of this case. Had Moses done so, it might have been considered his own judgment only.

The decision came quickly, "The man shall be surely put to death." Num. 15:35. That settled the question. The Sabbath commandment took its place with the other commandments. Its transgression was as serious as that of the others. Men might not so consider it. But God had spoken. The lesson is for us as well as for them. Let no one speak lightly of the Sabbath or defiantly transgress its precept.

Ezekiel's Story of the Exodus

When Moses wrote the story of the Exodus, he did not say all that might be said. Many years later, God, through the prophet Ezekiel, supplemented the account with some detailed information that is of value for our present study.

Ezekiel lived at the time of the beginning of the Babylonian captivity. Some of the people of Israel had already been carried into captivity, and others would soon follow. This was because of their sins—the same sins of which they had been guilty in Egypt and in the wilderness.

Certain elders came to Ezekiel to inquire of the Lord. This was a common custom in Israel. When there were matters in which they needed special guidance and instruction from God, the elders would appear before the prophet, asking him if he had any light from the Lord on the subject. In this case there was no hesitation in the answer. "As I live, saith the Lord, I will not be inquired of by you." Eze. 20:3.

The Lord now proceeds to tell them why He will not be inquired of by them. This leads Him to go into detail about what their fathers had done, and why He could not help them. The inference was that He could not help Israel now for the same reason that He could not help Israel then.

75

God begins the story by telling of the time when Israel was in cruel bondage in Egypt and prayed for deliverance. As a condition for helping them, God, through Moses, called to them, "Cast ye away every man the abominations of his eyes, and defile not yourselves with the idols of Egypt." Eze. 20:7.

But Israel would not hear. They wanted to be delivered, but not at such cost. They rebelled against God and did not cast away their idols. God therefore decided not only that He would not help them, but that He would punish them in the land of Egypt and leave them there. But God, in His mercy and for His name's sake, took pity on them and brought them out of the land of Egypt, that His name "should not be polluted before the heathen." Verses 8, 9.

Through the interposition of God, Israel experienced wonderful deliverance at the Red Sea and came into the wilderness of Sinai. It might be thought that they would now be ready to cast away their idols and serve the Lord with all their heart. But they were still rebellious. God bore long with them and patiently instructed them. "I caused them to go forth out of the land of Egypt," He says, "and brought them into the wilderness. And I gave them My statutes, and showed them My judgments, which if a man do, he shall even live in them. Moreover also I gave them My Sabbaths, to be a sign between Me and them, that they might know that I am the Lord that sanctify them." Verses 10-12. This was at Sinai.

The Sabbath in its essential nature is a sign of sanctification. A man may be disrespectful of his parents without being guilty of adultery. He may covet his neighbor's goods and yet not make any graven image. He may have great temptation along one line and very little along another line. But not so with Sabbathbreaking.

Violation of the Sabbath commandment is not so much

sin, as such, as it is a symptom that reveals an attitude that touches all the commandments. Sabbathbreaking in its essential nature is a rejection of God, a species of rebellion. It is not like killing or stealing or committing adultery. It reveals an inner state of disobedience; and disobedience is the essence of all sin.

Contrariwise, obedience to the Sabbath command shows a willingness of spirit that reaches far beyond the specific commandment into the very heart of religion, which in its essence is obedience. The man, therefore, who keeps the Sabbath holy does more than keep one of the commandments of God. He arrays himself on the side of obedience and law, regardless of any ulterior motive, and thus measures up to God's standard of what a man should be.

Israel neither understood nor appreciated the gift which God gave them in the Sabbath. As they had rebelled against God in Egypt, so they rebelled against Him in the wilderness. They did not walk in His statutes, and did not keep His law and His Sabbath. "They despised My judgments, which if a man do, he shall even live in them; and My Sabbaths they greatly polluted." Eze. 20:13.

We have no record either here or in the books of Moses of the way in which Israel polluted the Sabbath. They doubtless refrained from work on that day, especially after punishment had been meted out to the transgressor who gathered sticks on Sabbath. But Sabbathkeeping is more than abstinence from work. A man may abstain from work on the seventh day and yet not enter into the rest of God.

A man who rests on the seventh day, but whose hands are not clean and whose heart is not pure, defiles the Sabbath of the Lord, and makes the same mistake as did Israel in thinking that entering literal Canaan exhausted God's promise. Too many of them took Egypt along when they entered Canaan, and thus frustrated the plan of God.

God meant for them to leave Egypt behind, and as they entered Canaan enter into a new experience in God. All Israel did was to enter the land; but in doing so they neither received the promise nor entered the rest of God.

Israel kept the day, but the spiritual experience which should have been theirs, they entirely missed. They abstained from labor, but they did not enter into God's rest; they did not cease from their own works as God did from His. Their hearts were not changed.

This emphasizes the statement that the Sabbath is a sign of sanctification, and that no one who is not sanctified can keep the Sabbath as God would have it kept. It must ever be had in mind that true Sabbathkeeping includes a pure heart and a holy life. Whoever does not have those pollutes the Sabbath, however careful he may be in abstaining from work on the day.

Rebellion of Israel

Twice already Israel had rebelled, first in Egypt, and then in the wilderness. God remonstrated with them, but they would not hear; nor would they cast away their idols. He therefore proposed to destroy Israel and pour out His "fury upon them in the wilderness, to consume them." But again God did not carry out His plan, lest His name "be polluted before the heathen, in whose sight I brought them out." Eze. 20:14. So God spared them once more.

However, Israel came so far short of God's ideal and purpose, that He determined not to bring them "into the land which I had given them, . . . because they despised My judgments, and walked not in My statutes, but polluted My Sabbaths." Verses 15, 16. As a result of this decision, Israel was left to wander in the wilderness until the generation died which had come out of Egypt.

Having thus dealt with the fathers whom He had brought out of Egypt, He now addressed the younger generation, the children. They had seen what had happened to their elders, and should have been warned by their example. God "said unto their children in the wilderness, Walk ye not in the statutes of your fathers, neither observe their judgments, nor defile yourselves with their idols. I am the Lord your God; walk in My statutes, and keep My judgments, and do them; and hallow My Sabbaths; and they shall be a sign between Me and you, that ye may know that I am the Lord your God." Verses 18-20.

But the children had learned nothing from the experience of their fathers. "They walked not in My statutes, neither kept My judgments to do them, which if a man do, he shall even live in them; they polluted My Sabbaths: then I said, I would pour out My fury upon them, to accomplish My anger against them in the wilderness." Verse 21.

God's patience is now at an end, and He proclaims that He will scatter Israel "among the heathen, and disperse them through the countries; because they had not executed My judgments, but had despised My statutes, and had polluted My Sabbaths, and their eyes were after their fathers' idols." Verses 23, 24.

A Lesson for Israel in Captivity

As noted above, when the elders came to inquire of Ezekiel, many had already been carried captive to Babylon, and the rest would soon follow. They were eager to know God's mind, and for this reason they had sent a deputation to the prophet to hear what God had to say. This gave the Lord an opportunity to rehearse to them the story of the deliverance of their fathers from Egyptian bondage, and their experiences in entering the Promised Land.

Israel was now in a parallel situation. As their fathers were in slavery in Egypt, so Israel was now about to go into captivity in Babylon. As God formerly had delivered Israel out of Egypt, so Israel now asked to be delivered out of Babylon. The sins that afflicted Israel in Egypt were the same sins that afflicted Israel now, and the conditions of salvation and delivery were also the same. What God asked of Israel of old, He asked of the present Israel. For this reason God carefully rehearsed Israel's history for the benefit of the elders that came to inquire of the Lord, and told them in detail where the fathers had come short and wherein they had sinned.

The charges which God placed against Israel may be listed as follows:

1. They had failed to cast away the abomination of their eyes, and had defiled themselves with the idols of Egypt. This doubtless had reference to the filthy and obscene rites of the impure phallic worship which was at that time prominent in Egypt.

2. They had not walked in God's statutes, but had despised His judgments. This is what is referred to as rebellion, a general state of disinclination to do the will of God as well as of active opposition.

3. They had greatly polluted God's Sabbaths. This is emphasized four times, in Ezekiel 20:13, 16, 21, 24. In addition, the Sabbath is mentioned two times as a sign of sanctification and of the knowledge of God. Verses 12, 20.

After God has thus informed the elders of the transgressions of Israel of old, He now tells them that they are no better than their fathers, and that He will not be inquired of by them, but will bring them into "the wilderness of the people," and "purge out from among" them "the rebels," and not permit them to enter the land of Israel. Verses 35, 38. On the other hand, those who turn to the Lord, He will accept, "and I will be sanctified in you before the heathen." Verse 41. The failure of present Israel He lays directly on the leaders, the prophets and priests. "Her priests have violated My law, and have profaned Mine holy things: they have put no difference between the holy and profane, neither have they showed difference between the unclean and the clean, and have hid their eyes from My Sabbaths, and I am profaned among them. Her princes in the midst thereof are like wolves ravening the prey, to shed blood, and to destroy souls, to get dishonest gain. And her prophets have daubed them with untempered mortar, seeing vanity, and divining lies unto them, saying, Thus saith the Lord God, when the Lord hath not spoken." Eze. 22:26-28.

From Ezekiel we thus get a clear account of the reasons why Israel of old did not please God, why they died in the wilderness, and why the children also failed. They had forsaken the Lord for Egyptian idols, had refused to walk in God's statutes, had despised His judgments, and above all had polluted the Sabbath, which from the very beginning had been God's sign of sanctification.

Jeremiah's Message

Israel failed miserably in coming up to God's expectation at the time of the exodus from Egypt. They had now come to the time of another test in their imminent Babylonian bondage. Nebuchadnezzar's army had already carried many into captivity, and their beautiful city had been laid waste.

Again and again God had, through the prophets, sent word to them that if they would turn to the Lord with their whole heart and repent of their evil the Lord would be gracious to them. He had called their attention to the Sabbath and to the great and wonderful promises given them on condition of obedience.

Hear these words from Jeremiah, one of the last messages that came to them before they were finally carried away into captivity:

"Thus saith the Lord: Take heed to yourselves, and bear no burden on the Sabbath day, nor bring it in by the gates of Jerusalem; neither carry forth a burden out of your houses on the Sabbath day, neither do ye any work, but hallow ye the Sabbath day, as I commanded your fathers. But they obeyed not, neither inclined their ear, but made their neck stiff, that they might not hear, nor receive instruction. And it shall come to pass, if ye diligently hearken unto Me, saith the Lord, to bring in no burden through the gates of this city on the Sabbath day, but hallow the Sabbath day, to do no work therein; then shall there enter into the gates of this city kings and princes sitting upon the throne of David, riding in chariots and on horses, they, and their princes, the men of Judah, and the inhabitants of Jerusalem: and this city shall remain forever. And they shall come from the cities of Judah, and from the places about Jerusalem, and from the land of Benjamin, and from the plain, and from the mountains, and from the south, bringing burnt offerings, and sacrifices, and meat offerings, and incense, and bringing sacrifices of praise, unto the house of the Lord. But if ye will not heaken unto Me to hallow the Sabbath day, and not to bear a burden, even entering in at the gates of Jerusalem on the Sabbath day; then will I kindle a fire in the gates thereof, and it shall devour the palaces of Jerusalem, and it shall not be quenched." Jer. 17:21-27.

This, as stated, was one of the last messages sent to Israel before Nebuchadnezzar finally laid waste the city, destroyed the temple, and carried the remnant Israel captive into a strange country, there to become servants of a heathen people until they should have learned the lesson.

Nehemiah's Message

It would seem that by this time Israel should have known what the Lord required of them, and learned to follow His counsel. Their fathers had wandered forty years in the wilderness and at last died without entering the Promised Land. Now Israel was carried into Babylon for the same transgressions of which their fathers had been guilty. Ezekiel had faithfully rehearsed the history of Israel's failure; Jeremiah had added his warning; but all to no avail. And now they were in captivity.

Seventy years was the allotted time for this captivity— time for all the old men to die who were grown when the captivity began. The time had come to bring Israel back, and God kept His promise. Israel was permitted to leave Babylon and return to their land. Great was the rejoicing of the people as they once more set foot on their own soil and could resume the interrupted temple worship. Surely by this time they should have learned their lesson.

But they had not. In Babylon they had intermarried with the Babylonians, and had learned their heathen customs. In particular had they become careless with reference to the Sabbath, the very point on which they had been warned again and again. Nehemiah, who had been specially selected of God to lead the people, records the situation in these words:

"In those days saw I in Judah some treading wine presses on the Sabbath, and bringing in sheaves, and lading asses; as also wine, grapes, and figs, and all manner of burdens, which they brought into Jerusalem on the Sabbath day: and I testified against them in the day wherein they sold victuals. There dwelt men of Tyre also therein, which brought fish, and all manner of ware, and sold on the Sabbath unto the children of Judah, and in Jerusalem. Then I contended with the nobles of Judah, and said unto them, What evil thing is this that ye do, and profane the Sabbath day? Did not your fathers thus, and did not our God bring all this evil upon us, and upon this city? yet ye bring more wrath upon Israel by profaning the Sabbath.

And it came to pass, that when the gates of Jerusalem began to be dark before the Sabbath, I commanded that the gates should be shut, and charged that they should not be opened till after the Sabbath: and some of my servants set I at the gates, that there should no burden be brought in on the Sabbath day. So the merchants and sellers of all kind of ware lodged without Jerusalem once or twice. Then I testified against them, and said unto them, Why lodge ye about the wall? if ye do so again, I will lay hands on you. From that time forth came they no more on the Sabbath. And I commanded the Levites that they should cleanse themselves, and that they should come and keep the gates, to sanctify the Sabbath day. Remember me, O my God, concerning this also, and spare me according to the greatness of Thy mercy." Neh. 13:15-22.

Some of the children of Israel were "treading the wine press on the Sabbath, and bringing in sheaves, and lading asses;" others brought their burdens "into Jerusalem on the Sabbath," and "sold victuals." Nehemiah remonstrated with them and said that these were the things that had brought God's wrath upon them. "Did not your fathers thus," he reasons, "and did not our God bring all this evil upon us, and upon this city? Yet ye bring more wrath upon Israel by profaning the Sabbath." He thereupon ordered the gates of the city closed on the Sabbath, and even threatened to "lay hands on" those who persisted in transgression. At last the buyers and sellers came "no more on the Sabbath," and the Levites were invited to "come and keep the gates, to sanctify the Sabbath."

It is evident, of course, that this kind of forced Sabbath-keeping was not after God's order. To Him the Sabbath was a sign of sanctification, and without a life of holiness, the Sabbath became an empty ceremony that could never substitute for true sanctification.

Subsequent History

From the subsequent history of the Jews it appears that the Babylonian captivity and the remonstrances of the prophets at last made some impression on the people. They appear finally to have understood that their failure to keep the Sabbath had been the cause of their calamities from earliest times. They read the history of God's proving Israel in the wilderness, of how He rained manna from heaven for forty years, and taught them concerning the Sabbath. They read Ezekiel's account as he repeated to them the history of Israel's later failure. They read of Jeremiah's appeal to them to keep the Sabbath and the blessing that would come to them if they should do so. They learned from this that national greatness would never be theirs unless they kept the Sabbath; but that if they did, kings and princes should come to them, and Jerusalem should stand forever. They knew that God would do just as He said; for had they not been carried into captivity? Had not their city and their temple been burned, and had not God released them from their captivity at the end of the seventy years, as He promised? Now Nehemiah had once more warned them, and at last they woke up. From now on they would be faithful; they would do all that God required of them, and especially would they be careful of the Sabbath.

And careful they were. The Babylonian captivity marks a definite change in Israel. Nevermore did they turn to idols; nevermore did they make of the Sabbath a common working day. If it was as important as they were told, they would hedge it about with all kinds of restrictions. If their national existence and the blessing of God depended upon their faithfulness in observing the Sabbath, they would certainly keep it.

The mistake they now made was as fatal as the mistake

they had formerly made. They began to consider the Sabbath a means of salvation, both peronal and national, instead of a sign of sanctification. God wanted a holy people, and the Sabbath was to be the sign of this. Now they stressed the sign which could only be of little value without the accompanying reality of holiness.

Christ did His best to restore to Israel the Sabbath as God originally had given it to them, to be a blessing rather than a burden. He did not need to stress strictness in the minutia of Sabbathkeeping, for Israel had already gone too far in that direction. With their new viewpoint, the people, and especially the Pharisees, believed Christ to be slack in the observance of the Sabbath. They did not understand that He was attempting to show them its real purpose; that doing good, healing the sick, and committing acts of mercy on the Sabbath were pleasing in the sight of God, rather than merely mechanically observing the day.

Thus did Israel in the time of Christ fail as completely as had ancient Israel in understanding the true meaning of the Sabbath. They failed in a different way, it is true, but they failed as definitely. It is this to which the writer of Hebrews refers when he warns his fellow believers not to fall after the same manner of unbelief.

The Message of Hebrews

The writer of Hebrews follows the same method that Ezekiel had previously followed; namely, calling attention to the history of Israel when they came out of Egypt. He mentions the fact that God was provoked and grieved with them, though they "saw My works forty years." Because of their unbelief, their "carcasses fell in the wilderness," and God sware "that they should not enter into His rest." Heb. 3:9-18.

Having called attention to the failure of the fathers and the reason for it, he issues a warning to his own generation. "Let us therefore fear," he says, "lest, a promise being left us of entering into His rest, any of you should seem to come short of it." Heb. 4:1. Israel failed; now see to it that you do not fail, is his argument. "They could not enter in because of unbelief." Heb. 3:19.

The writer now attempts to make clear that entering into the earthly Canaan and entering into God's rest are not the same thing. There were many who entered Canaan who did not enter into rest. Joshua, indeed, brought them into the Promised *Land,* but he did not bring them into the promised *rest* of God.

When Israel entered Canaan, they felt that they had attained their goal. But this was not God's idea. The rest of which He spoke, and into which He would conduct them, was the rest from sin, rest from their own works. Of this Canaan was a symbol, as was also the Sabbath. To rest on the seventh day from their labor was good, and to enter Canaan was according to God's command; but good as these were, they were only symbolic of something higher—of rest from sin, rest from one's own labor, rest in God, of which the Sabbath was symbolic.

"We which have believed do enter into rest;" that is, we who are converted have the true rest, rest in God. Heb. 4:3. This rest in God, this freedom from and victory over sin, the writer closely connects with the works "finished from the foundation of the world. For He spake in a certain place of the seventh day on this wise, And God rested the seventh day from all His work." Heb. 4:3, 4.

In a most beautiful and effective way the writer thus connects the seventh-day Sabbath with the true rest of God. Joshua had brought Israel into the Promised Land, but he had not given them rest, for only he has truly entered into rest who "hath ceased from his own works as God did from His." This rest is a spiritual rest, a rest from our "own works," a ceasing from sin. It is to this rest that

God calls His people, and it is of this rest that both the Sabbath and Canaan are symbols.

The mere entering of the land of Canaan did not exhaust God's promise of rest. Nor does the mere keeping of the Sabbath do this. The Sabbath is, indeed, a sign of sanctification. But the sign must never be substituted for the reality, nor, on the other hand, must it be ignored. The writer of Hebrews is anxious that his hearers shall not make the same mistake that Israel of old made. He wants them to enter in, and not "fall after the same manner of unbelief."

"There remaineth therefore a rest to the people of God." Heb. 4:9. The original Greek as well as the margin and the Revised Version has, "There remaineth therefore a keeping of a Sabbath to the people of God." Verse 9.

There can be no mistaking the intent of the argument of the writer of Hebrews. Israel of old failed; they disregarded God's statutes and laws, and especially they polluted the Sabbath. When Israel rejected the Sabbath, they rejected that for which it stands, holiness of life. They entered into Canaan, but they did not enter into God's rest, nor into life. Hence God's purpose had not been fulfilled. So God issued other calls, and even after Israel had entered Canaan, He called upon them to enter into His rest, "saying in David, Today, after so long a time, as it is said, Today if ye will hear His voice, harden not your hearts." Verse 7. That same call has sounded to every generation since then, and the writer of the Hebrews was now sounding the last call that would ever go to Israel as a nation. A very short time after this book was written, the temple was finally destroyed, and no more calls were issued. Israel as a nation had had its last call.

In this argument in Hebrews the reader will not fail to note the introduction of the seventh-day Sabbath. "God did rest the seventh day from all His works." Heb. 4:4.

"The works were finished from the foundation of the world." Verse 3. "There remaineth therefore a keeping of a Sabbath to the people of God." Verse 9, margin. "He that is entered into His rest, he also hath ceased from his own works, as God did from His." Verse 10. All this sums up into a telling and effective argument for the seventh-day Sabbath in the New Testament. It should be remembered, however, that telling as this argument is for the seventh day, there is as definite danger now as then that the sign be substituted for that for which it is a sign. God demands holiness of life. Of this the Sabbath is a sign. We must not reject the sign, much less reject that for which it stands. Let all consider this. It is vital.

Christ and the Law

THE most precious document in the possession of mankind is the law of God contained in the ten commandments. It was spoken by God Himself in majesty upon Mt. Sinai, confirmed by Christ while on earth, and given to the church and the world as a guide of life and standard of conduct. Its clear, crisp, decisive commands comprehend the whole duty of man. In its original form it is the constitution of the universe; as adapted to man it defines his every duty. It is the foundation of all human law, the bulwark of society and civilization, the protector of liberty, the guardian of morality, the preserver of the home, the security of the state. Obeyed, it brings happiness, prosperity, and peace; disobeyed or ignored, it brings sorrow, disaster, and chaos. Men and nations have disregarded it; pew and pulpit have attempted to disannul it; evil men and seducers have violated it; society has flouted it; yet it remains the one accepted standard of conduct; and mankind, whether they approve of it or not, pay it lip service. It is a builder of character, a reprover of sin, a guide of life.

The Law of God

"God spake all these words, saying,

"I am the Lord thy God, which have brought thee out of the land of Egypt, out of the house of bondage."

1. "Thou shalt have no other gods before Me."

2. "Thou shalt not make unto thee any graven image, or any likeness of anything that is in heaven above, or that is in the earth beneath, or that is in the water under the earth: thou shalt not bow down thyself to them, nor serve them: for I the Lord thy God am a jealous God, visiting the iniquity of the fathers upon the children unto the third and fourth generation of them that hate Me; and showing mercy unto thousands of them that love Me, and keep My commandments."

3. "Thou shalt not take the name of the Lord thy God in vain; for the Lord will not hold him guiltless that taketh His name in vain."

4. "Remember the Sabbath day, to keep it holy. Six days shalt thou labor, and do all thy work: but the seventh day is the Sabbath of the Lord thy God: in it thou shalt not do any work, thou, nor thy son, nor thy daughter, thy manservant, nor thy maidservant, nor thy cattle, nor thy stranger that is within thy gates: for in six days the Lord made heaven and earth, the sea, and all that in them is, and rested the seventh day: wherefore the Lord blessed the Sabbath day, and hallowed it."

5. "Honor thy father and thy mother: that thy days may be long upon the land which the Lord thy God giveth thee."

6. "Thou shalt not kill."

7. "Thou shalt not commit adultery."

8. "Thou shalt not steal."

9. "Thou shalt not bear false witness against thy neighbor."

10. "Thou shalt not covet thy neighbor's house, thou shalt not covet thy neighbor's wife, nor his manservant, nor his maidservant, nor his ox, nor his ass, nor anything that is thy neighbor's."   Ex. 20:1-17.

Thus read the "ten words" spoken by God Himself amid the thunder and lightnings of Sinai.

Christ and the Law

By many of His contemporaries Christ was considered a radical; especially was this true of the Pharisees, who continually dogged His footsteps, ready to catch any phrase from His lips that might be construed against Him.

The Pharisees were accustomed to have great deference paid to them and their opinions by the people. Christ, however, did not seem impressed by them, and did not show them the respect which they thought was their due. They had tried repeatedly to entrap Him in words, but each time they were worsted and lost prestige in the eyes of the people. He had a disconcerting way of turning the question back at them. They were not "able to answer Him a word, neither durst any man from that day forth ask Him any more questions." Matt. 22:46. They did not enjoy being humiliated, especially before the people. At last they decided to ask no more questions.

This situation did not make the scribes and the Pharisees love Jesus. They hated Him, and were willing to do almost anything to destroy His influence with the people, for "the people gladly received Him: for they were all waiting for Him." Luke 8:40. However, they had hopes that in the matter of the law they might find the occasion they sought. As the conspirators of old said of Daniel, "We shall not find any occasion against this Daniel, except we find it against him concerning the law of his God" (Dan. 6:5), so these hoped that when Christ declared Himself on the law, He would furnish the occasion that would lay Him open to the charges they were anxious to place against Him.

Christ was never neutral or negative. His statements were unequivocal. They not only could be understood, but they could not be misunderstood. He was straightforward, clear cut, positive, dynamic. People always knew where He stood. He did not attempt to gain popular favor by flattery or by lowering standards. Sin was sin to Him, and He called it by that name. It was these traits in Christ which the Pharisees hoped would make it easier for them to find some accusation against Him that would count with the people.

The Jews were great sticklers for the law. Especially were the Pharisees observant of the letter of the law and intolerant of such as did not or could not measure up to their requirements of observance. They had added many ordinances since God first gave the law, and it was a life study to know what was required. It was impossible for the common people to have this exact and comprehensive knowledge; hence they were unable to reach the standard set. The Pharisees held that the "people who knoweth not the law are cursed." John 7:49.

Under these circumstances it was of great interest to the Jews and especially to the Pharisees, to know Jesus' attitude toward the law. As a teacher it was incumbent upon Him to make His position known and tell the people plainly where He stood. It was in this announcement that the Pharisees hoped to entrap Him, for they knew He was outspoken and would not leave them in doubt regarding His position.

Jesus did not disappoint them. In His first recorded sermon He dealt exhaustively with the law, and made His position known. Nine blessings He pronounced upon the poor, the mourners, the meek, the hungry and thirsty, the merciful, the pure, the peacemakers, the persecuted, the reviled; then He said:

"Ye are the salt of the earth: but if the salt have lost his savor, wherewith shall it be salted? it is thenceforth good for nothing, but to be cast out, and to be trodden under foot of men. Ye are the light of the world. A city that is set on a hill cannot be hid. Neither do men light a candle, and put it under a bushel, but on a candlestick; and it giveth light unto all that are in the house. Let your light so shine before men, that they may see your good works, and glorify your Father which is in heaven.

"Think not that I am come to destroy the law, or the prophets: I am not come to destroy, but to fulfill. For verily I say unto you, Till heaven and earth pass, one jot or one tittle shall in no wise pass from the law, till all be fulfilled. Whosoever therefore shall break one of these least commandments, and shall teach men so, he shall be called least in the kingdom of heaven: but whosoever shall do and teach them, the same shall be called great in the kingdom of heaven." Matt. 5:13-19.

Jesus knew what was in men's hearts and what they were thinking. Answering their unspoken thoughts, He said, "Think not that I am come to destroy the law, or the prophets." This was the very thing the Pharisees were thinking. Had they not seen Him do the unprecedented thing of driving out the buyers and sellers from the temple? Had they not seen Him make a scourge of small cords, overthrow the tables, and scatter the money of the changers? Had He not spoken of the temple as His Father's house? John 2:13-17. If He *began* His work that way, what might the end be? Evidently He was a radical that would bear watching. He seemed to have little respect for the temple appointments. Was He attempting to destroy the law and the prophets? With great interest all had been awaiting His pronouncement on the law. And now they had it. He was not abolishing the law. He was standing by it. Not even a tittle or a jot should fail. He was not destroying it, as some had feared. He was fulfilling it.

"Think not that I am come to destroy the law, or the prophets. I am not come to destroy, but to fulfill." The law here mentioned is, broadly speaking, the writings of

Moses, but specifically the moral law, the ten command-ments, from which the writings of Moses primarily de-rived their name. By "the prophets" are meant the writ-ings of the prophets, such as are in the Old Testament.

Some hold that the law here mentioned is only the Old Testament and does not specifically refer to the ten com-mandments. But that it means more than merely the writings of Moses in general is evident from the illustra-tions which Jesus proceeds to give.

"Ye have heard that it was said to them of old time, Thou shalt not kill; and whosoever shall kill shall be in danger of the judgment: but I say unto you, that everyone who is angry with his brother shall be in danger of the judgment; and whosoever shall say to his brother, Raca, shall be in danger of the council; and whosoever shall say, Thou fool, shall be in danger of the hell of fire. If there-fore thou art offering thy gift at the altar, and there re-memberest that thy brother hath aught against thee, leave there thy gift before the altar, and go thy way, first be reconciled to thy brother, and then come and offer thy gift. Agree with thine adversary quickly, while thou art with him in the way; lest haply the adversary deliver thee to the judge, and the judge deliver thee to the officer, and thou be cast into prison. Verily I say unto thee, Thou shalt by no means come out thence, till thou have paid the last farthing.

"Ye have heard that it was said, Thou shalt not commit adultery: but I say unto you, that everyone that looketh on a woman to lust after her hath committed adultery with her already in his heart. And if thy right eye causeth thee to stumble, pluck it out, and cast it from thee: for it is profitable for thee that one of thy members should perish, and not thy whole body be cast into hell. And if thy right hand causeth thee to stumble, cut it off, and cast it from thee: for it is profitable for thee that one of thy members should perish, and not thy whole body go into hell. It was said also, Whosoever shall put away his wife, let him give her a writing of divorcement: but I say unto you, that everyone that putteth away his wife, saving for the cause of fornication, maketh her an adulteress: and whosoever shall marry her when she is put away committeth adultery." Matt. 5:21-32, R. V.

Jesus here selects two of the ten commandments to show how He fulfills the law. The commandment, "Thou shalt not kill," He explains, has a deeper meaning than that of merely taking the life of a man. Whoever hates his brother has taken the first step in transgression. In saying this, Christ corrects the conception which some had that the keeping of the commandments was merely an outward compliance which did not touch the inward state of the heart. He interprets the law as being definitely spiritual, as having application to the mind and heart, rather than being a mere rule of outward conduct.

This He emphasizes again in His interpretation of the seventh commandment, "Thou shalt not commit adultery." Men may transgress this commandment in their minds as well as by an overt act; and the one is as surely a transgression as the other.

From these interpretations we are on sure ground when we hold that the law here mentioned in a specific and definite way refers to the ten commandments. So far from Christ's destroying this law, He magnifies it, shows its far-reaching character, and announces that he who transgresses it even in thought "shall be in danger of the hell of fire." Matt. 5:22, R. V. Christ left no doubt in the mind of any regarding where He stood on the law. He took His stand squarely on the ten commandments, saying that "one jot or one tittle shall in no wise pass from the law, till all be fulfilled." Whoever should break one of the least of the commandments, and teach men so, should be called the least in the kingdom of heaven; while he who should do and teach them should be called great.

It is incumbent upon every teacher of religion to declare himself on the law. Men have a right to know whether the religion he teaches has a background of law and order, or if it is one of those irresponsible movements that demand privileges but shun responsibilities. Especially in these days, when lawlessness prevails, should the position of every religious movement on the question of law be made clear. Christ defined His position at the outset of His career. Every religious teacher should do the same.

Christ and the Pharisees

When Christ took the two commandments, "Thou shalt not kill" and "Thou shalt not commit adultery," and showed their spiritual application, He was fulfilling that which had been prophesied of Him: "The Lord is well pleased for His righteousness' sake; *He will magnify the law, and make it honorable.*" Isa. 42:21. The context shows this to be a definite Messianic prophecy. Christ thus fulfilled this prophecy. He lifted the law out of the mass of petty restrictions with which the scribes and Pharisees had encumbered it, and restored it to its rightful place. No one need be fearful that Christ came to destroy the law. On the contrary, He came to magnify it, to make it honorable. The Pharisees, by their multitudinous rules, belittled it and made it ridiculous.

The Two Commandments

Consider the two commandments which Christ used by way of illustration, doubtless for a purpose.

"Thou shalt not kill." There were those among the Pharisees who habitually carried a broom with which to sweep a path before them, lest haply they should step on some insect or worm and kill it. Their hearts might be filled with hatred of Christ, they might even at this very time be planning to take the life of One who had come from heaven to show them the way of salvation, but this did not hinder them from ostentatiously carrying their broom and exhibiting their righteousness before men. In doing this they were giving people an altogether wrong conception of the meaning of the law. They, as well as the people, needed someone to show them its real meaning, to fulfill its demands. This Christ did. All who heard Christ's explanation of the sixth commandment knew ever after that if they were to keep the law, they would have to watch their thinking; that it was not enough to carry a broom; that it was the heart that counted; and that hatred was a transgression of the law. In their heart of hearts they knew that Christ was right and the Pharisees were wrong.

"Thou shalt not commit adultery." This was the other commandment to which Christ called attention and which He used as an illustration. The Pharisees were not unaware of the spiritual values of the law—and this knowledge was their condemnation. They well knew that God required "truth in the inward parts," and that the "sacrifices of God are a broken spirit: a broken and a contrite heart, O God, Thou wilt not despise." Ps. 51:6, 17. But they chose to ignore these counsels and to confine their religious activities to that which could be seen and appreciated by men, from whom they might receive praise. Lest they be tempted to lust after a woman, some would blindfold themselves, and thus think themselves safe—as willful a perversion of the intent of the law as could be imagined. Christ unmasked all this hypocrisy when He stated that "within, out of the heart of men, proceed evil thoughts, adulteries, fornications, murders, thefts, covetousness, wickedness, deceit, lasciviousness, an evil eye, blasphemy, pride, foolishness: all these things come from within, and defile the man." Mark 7:21-23.

When Christ interpreted these two commandments, He was in effect saying: "God looks on the heart. The law is holy and just and good. Be careful of even the smallest infractions. Every jot and tittle counts. But do not get the idea that outward obedience is all that the law requires. It demands purity of thought as well as of life. It is spiritual in its intent. I am come to magnify the law and make it honorable." "Except your righteousness shall exceed the righteousness of the scribes and Pharisees, ye shall in no case enter into the kingdom of heaven."

Christ's words must have cut the Pharisees to the quick. They were proud of their reputation for legal exactitude. They paid tithe of mint, anise, and cumin. Some of them fasted twice in the week. They thanked God that they were not like other sinners. They made broad the phylacteries, made long prayers, and compassed sea and land to make a proselyte. And now Christ said in the hearing of the multitude, that unless their righteousness exceeded that of the Pharisees, they would in no case enter into the kingdom. Later on in His ministry He told the chief priests and the elders "that the publicans and the harlots go into the kingdom of God before you." Matt. 21:31. No wonder the leaders of Israel looked askance at the young Galilean whom the people believed and followed, but who did not recognize the officials of the temple and the religious leaders, or give them the honor which they demanded.

If the Pharisees had hoped to find some cause of complaint against Christ in the matter of the law, they were disappointed. If they thought that He had come to destroy it—as seems evident from the form of Christ's pronouncement—or to change or abrogate it, they had entirely miscalculated His purpose. Their evil intent was frustrated, and they themselves stood exposed. Christ believed in the law. As the Pharisees were careful of the smallest matters, so Christ omitted no jot or tittle. If they stood by the law and the prophets, so did He. But in the conception of the nature of the law, Christ and the Pharisees were as widely separated as the east is from the west. To the Pharisees the law was a set of rules to direct the outward conduct of man, and by which they might judge others. To Christ the law was a spiritual counselor and friend, a guide, an aid to conscience, a mirror of the soul, a revealer of the will of God, a close ally of the Holy Spirit in convincing men of sin, of righteousness, and of judgment.

The Moral Law Spiritual

"We know that the law is spiritual," says Paul. Rom. 7:14. To this he adds by way of contrast, "But I am carnal, sold under sin." Paul had not always thought of himself as carnal, nor perhaps of the law as spiritual. He gave this testimony concerning himself before his conversion, "As touching the law, a Pharisee; concerning zeal, persecuting the church; touching the righteousness which is in the law, blameless." Phil. 3:5, 6. This was Paul's self-estimation. He was blameless as far as the law was concerned, as indeed all the Pharisees considered themselves. Their conduct was doubtless correct as regarded outward behavior, and with that they were satisfied. Paul was an exemplary young man, a good Pharisee. With the young man he could say, "All these things have I kept from my youth up." Matt. 19:20.

Paul's Experience

Paul, born in Tarsus, had been brought up at the feet of the great teacher, Gamaliel, in Jerusalem. Here, according to his own statement, he had been "taught according to the perfect manner of the law of the fathers." Acts

22:3. Nevertheless he considered it his duty to persecute the saints of God. "I imprisoned and beat in every synagogue them that believed on Thee," he recalls. Acts 22:19. "Many of the saints did I shut up in prison, having received authority from the chief priests, and when they were put to death, I gave my voice against them. And I punished them oft in every synagogue, and compelled them to blaspheme; and being exceedingly mad against them, I persecuted them even unto strange cities." Acts 26:10, 11. From this it is easy to see that though Paul had been "taught according to the perfect manner of the law," his understanding of the law was not perfect. It was necessary for him to get an entirely different opinion of himself as well as of the law.

This change in his experience came as he was on the way to Damascus to persecute the saints of God. At noon one day a great light suddenly shone from heaven, and Paul fell blind to the ground. He heard a voice which he recognized as that of Jesus of Nazareth, and this voice commanded him to proceed into the city, where he would be told what to do.

Three days of darkness followed, but then light broke upon his darkened soul, and the former persecutor became a follower of the lowly Nazarene. He thought he had been a good man. But now he saw himself in a different light. No longer was he the proud Pharisee who boasted of the law. He saw himself as a sinner who needed help and pardon. He fell on the Rock and was broken. Paul was a new man.

Up till this time Paul had considered himself blameless; he believed that he had kept the law and done all that it commanded. Now he saw himself in a new light, and not a very flattering one. He saw the spiritual aspects of the law as he had never seen them before, and he also saw himself as carnal—a view that he had not had previously.

This change was brought about by the Spirit of God, who used as a means the tenth commandment. Paul expresses it thus: "I had not known sin, but by the law: for I had not known lust, except the law had said, Thou shalt not covet." Rom. 7:7.

The full force of this commandment had not occurred to him before. He had been careful of his conduct; he had been "blameless" in the law. But now the command, "Thou shalt not covet," struck him full force. It dawned on him that the commandments take cognizance not only of the outward and overt acts, but of the thoughts and intents of the heart. He had been able to control his outward behavior, but his thinking revealed to him a state of heart for which he knew no remedy. The Jewish sacrificial law provided a sacrifice for whoever had transgressed the law unwittingly. But there was no remedy provided for any whose thinking was wrong. A man might be forgiven for stealing if he was willing to restore what he had taken, and add a fifth part to the ill-gotten gain, and bring the requisite offering. Lev. 6:1-7. But there was no provision for the man who coveted. He might be forgiven as we are now forgiven, but there was *no provision in the law of Moses* for this. For sins of this nature he must go to the Lord direct.

A Spiritual Law

It was the commandment, "Thou shalt not covet," which made Paul appreciate the spiritual nature of the law. He now understood that the law dealt not merely with outward conduct, but also with the heart. He now saw that there was no remedy for the sins of the mind but in Christ. He could now announce to the world his great discovery which had meant so much to him: "Be it known unto you therefore, men and brethren, that through this Man is preached unto you the forgiveness of sins: and by Him all that believe are justified from all things, *from which ye could not be justified by the law of Moses."* Acts 13:38, 39.

To covet is not an overt act of sin. It is not *doing* something wrong; it is *thinking* wrong. Covetousness is a state of mind; it is not *committing* the sin, but *wanting* to do it. The mind is the last thing that will be brought fully under control. Many people can control their outward behavior; they can even control their speech; but their minds run wild. In the midst of the most solemn meeting they are suddenly made aware of the deep-seated nature of sin. Thoughts which they would be ashamed to let their best friends know flit through the mind, and in anguish of spirit they cry out for help. While they know that they are not responsible for these wicked suggestions of Satan, they are horrified at the possibilities which they suggest. With a humble heart and a humble spirit they send a petition to the only One who can help them. They cry for a clean *heart;* they want the *fountain* cleansed. They get a new view of their need of help from on high, and they understand as never before that if the tree is corrupt, there is no way in which it may bear good fruit.

It was some such experience that came to Paul as he was considering the commandment, "Thou shalt not covet." He saw the abysmal depth of iniquity in his own heart. He thought that he had been blameless in the law; he thought that he had kept it; but when the commandment came, sin revived. He knew then that the law was spiritual, but that he was carnal. He had always considered the commandment to be holy, just, and good, and he also thought that he was holy, just, and good. "But when the commandment came, sin revived, and I died. And the commandment, which was ordained to life, I found to be unto death." Rom. 7:9, 10.

Those who today think lightly of the law have never thought very deeply about it, nor have they seen themselves in its light as Paul did. Two things Paul learned in his conversion: that the law is spiritual, and that he was carnal. Men as verily need that lesson today. Too many agree with Paul's estimate of himself, "touching the righteousness which is in the law, blameless." That was Paul's estimate, and that is their estimate, "blameless." They, and all of us, need a deeper look into their own hearts as well as into the abounding grace of God.

Let it be settled at once and for all that the law is spiritual. We must never conceive of God as being satisfied with outward righteousness only. God looks to the heart. He is interested in the inward man even more than in the outward. Hence His rule of conduct includes the whole man, body, soul, and spirit.

It was this conception of the law which Christ was eager that His hearers should receive as He made His first important address touching upon the law. Christ had been present when the law was announced in grandeur upon Mt. Sinai. He knew the deeply spiritual import of every statement in that law. He knew how completely inadequate in the sight of God is mere outward compliance with the requirements of the law, and He was deeply grieved that the teachers of His people should have such a low conception of the expressed will of God. He knew that all this must be changed. He therefore lost no time in declaring His position on the law.

The Place of the Law in the Teaching of Christ

Christ did not treat the law as a formal, cold, legal enactment. To Him it was the way of life, and not a series of prohibitions. He believed, as did Paul, that "the commandment . . . was ordained to life." Rom. 7:10. Of a full heart He could say: "I delight to do Thy will, O My God; yea, Thy law is within My heart." Ps. 40:8. He had inspired the psalmist to say: "I love Thy commandments above gold; yea, above fine gold," "and Thy law is my delight." "O how love I Thy law! it is my meditation all the day." "Thy testimonies are wonderful." "I will keep the commandments of my God." Ps. 119:127, 174, 97, 129, 115. That this conception was not mere sentiment with Christ, but a living reality, is evident from the way He applied the law to specific cases. Let us consider two of these.

The Young Man and the Lawyer

On a certain occasion a young man came to Jesus "and said unto Him, Good Master, what good thing shall I do, that I may have eternal life? And He said unto him, Why callest thou Me good? there is none good but one, that is, God: but if thou wilt enter into life, keep the commandments. He saith unto Him, Which? Jesus said, Thou shalt do no murder, Thou shalt not commit adultery, Thou shalt not steal, Thou shalt not bear false witness, Honor thy father and thy mother: and, Thou shalt love thy neighbor as thyself. The young man saith unto Him, All these things have I kept from my youth up: what lack I yet? Jesus said unto him, If thou wilt be perfect, go and sell that thou hast, and give to the poor, and thou shalt have treasure in heaven: and come and follow Me. But when the young man heard that saying, he went away sorrowful: for he had great possessions." Matt. 19:16-22.

Some may be a little perplexed at the answer which Jesus gave this young man when he asked what he should do to have eternal life. "Keep the commandments," Jesus said. When the man asked what commandments were meant, Jesus referred him to the law of God as contained in the ten precepts. Why did Jesus tell him this, when He might have told him to have faith, or to give his heart to God, or any one of the many things that are appropriate for such an occasion?

That this was not the only time Jesus answered in this way is evident from the record. On another occasion a lawyer stood up and asked: "Master, what shall I do to inherit eternal life?" Luke 10:25. To this Jesus answered: "What is written in the law? how readest thou? And he answering said, Thou shalt love the Lord thy God with all thy heart, and with all thy soul, and with all thy strength, and with all thy mind; and thy neighbor as thyself. And He said unto him, Thou hast answered right: this do, and thou shalt live." Luke 10:26-28.

It can hardly be supposed that Jesus treated their questions lightly and gave them answers not in harmony with the facts. But if this is really the answer to the question of how eternal life may be gained, how can we explain or justify the answer? It seems so at variance with the answer that most ministers of today would give, that some amplification or explanation is in order. If Jesus were here today, and a member of some ministerial association should ask Him how He would answer the question of how eternal life might be attained, and Jesus should answer now as He did then, would He be considered evangelical? It is highly probable that He would be asked to explain His answer.

We take it for granted that Jesus did not trifle with these men when so vital a matter as eternal life was concerned. We must believe that He gave them an honest answer, for certainly nothing less would be expected of Him. What, then, is implied in the answer? On this hangs much.

The lawyer, in reply to Jesus' question of how he read the law, had answered: "Thou shalt love the Lord thy God with all thy heart, and with all thy soul, and with all thy strength, and with all thy mind; and thy neighbor as thyself." Verse 27. The lawyer understood that the law demanded love to God and love to man. Christ said,

"Thou hast answered right: this do, and thou shalt live."

If we take Jesus' interpretation of the law as the law of love, may we not see light in the answer that Jesus gave? "Love is the fulfilling of the law." Rom. 13:10. God Himself is love. His law is love. Christ says: "If ye keep My commandments, ye shall abide in My love; even as I have kept My Father's commandments, and abide in His love." "Jesus answered and said unto him, If a man love Me, he will keep My words: and My Father will love him, and we will come unto him, and make our abode with him." "If ye love Me, keep My commandments." John 15:10; 14:23, 15.

Need of a New View

Apparently we need a new view of the law of God. It is not, as some call it, a yoke of bondage; it is not a hard taskmaster; it is not a bond of restraint. It is a glorious law of liberty, of love, of friendly guidance. It is God ordained, a transcript of His own character, the most precious thing in the sanctuary above, the foundation of the mercy seat and of the glorious plan of salvation. It is kept in the heart of Christ, free from any possible harm that might come to it. Ps. 40:8. It is the perfect embodiment of the will of God, the supreme rule of life. Why should any think lightly of it? It reflects the very heart and mind of the Almighty.

The law of love is the law of life. No man who does not love God can be saved. But "this is the love of God, that we keep His commandments." 1 John 5:3. No man can be saved who does not know God. But "he that saith, I know Him, and keepeth not His commandments, is a liar, and the truth is not in him." 1 John 2:4. No man can be saved who continues in sin. And "sin is the transgression of the law." 1 John 3:4. If, therefore, we are to be saved, we must love God and keep His commandments. If we say we love God, we must prove that love in the way God demands. We must stop transgressing the law; for "sin is the transgression of the law." At the conclusion of His work on earth, Christ could say: "I have kept My Father's commandments, and abide in His love." John 15:10. If we follow His example, we shall not go far astray.

With Christ's definition in mind that the law of God is the law of love, and that on this hang all the law and the prophets, we accept His statement of the law as the way of life. There is no other way. "He that loveth not knoweth not God; for God is love." 1 John 4:8. But to know God is life eternal. John 17:3. If, therefore, we do not know God unless we love, and the knowledge of God is eternal life, and the only way that "we do know that we know Him [is] if we keep His commandments," and this keeping of the commandments "is the love of God," we are again shut up to the proposition that the law of God plays a prominent part in our relationship to God. 1 John 2:3; 5:3. Only at the peril of our souls can we neglect it. Such was the teaching of Jesus, and, being the teaching of Jesus, it is also the teaching of all who follow Him.

Jesus and Tradition

Jesus had continual difficulty with the Jews over the subject of tradition. During the centuries of their existence, there had grown up among them many customs that with the passage of years had taken on the nature of law. The fathers had done certain things in a certain way, and succeeding generations followed the custom set. After a while it became a matter of disrespect to vary from the custom, which by that time had practically become law. The fathers were considered good men who followed God, and hence to follow them was in reality to follow God. The custom might be good or bad, but once it had become a settled practice, it came to be considered sin to vary in any way from the custom. It was only a tradition, but it was given all the force of a command of God.

Against this Jesus protested, and with good reason. For often the customs of the Jews contradicted the will of God as expressed in the law. Men accepted tradition and neglected the law. To Jesus it was immaterial whether the traditions in themselves were comparatively innocent or outright evil. If they in any way interfered with or made of none effect the law of God, He promptly set them aside.

The Washing of Hands

A case in point was the custom of washing the hands before eating. As practiced by the Jews, it was not an ordinance of cleanliness merely, but rather a ceremonial performance. The person would dip his hands in water, cupping them; he would then raise his hands and let the water run down to the elbow. This he would repeat several times, and the rite was over. Such an ordinance in itself cannot be considered very dangerous or subversive of the faith. It was one of the "added" precepts which the Jews considered very important. The Pharisees decided to make it a test case regarding Jesus' stand on tradition, and Jesus was perfectly willing to have it so.

The scribes and Pharisees had come down from Jerusalem to Galilee with a complaint about the disciples. They had omitted the ordinance of hand washing, and the Pharisees felt that the matter was of importance enough to call it to the attention of the Master. It was not merely zeal for the law which prompted them in this, though the complaint would have the effect of emphasizing their carefulness in adherence to tradition; their complaint would in itself constitute an indirect rebuke to Jesus for permitting His disciples to transgress tradition, and would compel Him to take His stand for or against the ordinance. Should He reject their complaint, they could report Him to the people as a violator of tradition. Should He admit the justice of the charge, they could boast of having set Him and His disciples right. This, of course, would prove that they knew more than He did about the law, and that they were stricter in its observance. In either case they would win out, and their reputation would be enhanced.

Jesus had just fed the five thousand, had miraculously crossed the sea by walking on the water, and was now engaged in healing the people. The sick lay by the hundreds in the streets, and as He passed they prayed that "they might touch if it were but the border of His garment: and as many as touched Him were made whole." Mark 6:56. The whole region, thousands upon thousands of people, pressed to get near the Master.

Jesus knew why the Pharisees had chosen this occasion to bring this question before Him. He knew that they wanted to expose Him before the people and make Him out to be a transgressor of their tradition. But not for a moment did He hesitate. He accepted their challenge, and was ready to declare Himself on tradition.

Jesus and the Pharisees

It was probably in the open square of the town that Jesus met the Pharisees. The people must have been deeply impressed with the fact that only a very important matter could have brought the Pharisees to undertake the long journey from Jerusalem. They thronged about Christ and the visitors, to learn the important message which these high officials had brought. It was with astonishment and some perplexity that they heard the Pharisees ask the apparently trivial question: "Why walk not Thy disciples according to the tradition of the elders, but eat bread with unwashen hands?" Mark 7:5.

Was this the question that had brought them on this long journey? Perhaps the matter was of greater importance than the people thought. Christ was doing a wonderful work in healing their sick. Whether or not the disciples washed their hands before eating did not seem to the simple fisherfolk of great importance. But perhaps they were mistaken. The learned scribes doubtless knew, and they seemed to think that washing the hands was most important. The question now was, What would be Jesus' attitude toward and reply to the accusation?

If the people had been astonished and perplexed at the accusation, they were dumfounded when they heard Jesus' answer: "Well hath Esaias prophesied of you hypocrites, as it is written, This people honoreth Me with their lips, but their heart is far from Me." Verse 6. They could hardly believe their ears.

Picture the scene. A dignified, solemn group of men, delegates from the highest authority among the Jews; a young teacher accused by them of permitting His disciples to transgress the traditions of the elders; thousands of people milling about to witness the scene; hundreds of sick awaiting the healing touch of the Master, and the work delayed until the question of hand washing was settled! And now in answer to the accusation come Christ's biting words: "You hypocrites"! What irreverence, what indignity, what boldness, of this young Galilean! Would the Pharisees immediately demand that He be apprehended and punished for thus humiliating them, who were leaders, in the sight of the people? But not a word did they say. Jesus completely commanded the situation.

"You hypocrites." What a terrific indictment. Ordinarily when a delegation of such men appeared from Jerusalem to call to account some false teacher, the miscreant would appear with trembling before the august inquisitors. Never had anyone dared so to address the leaders. The people could not understand why the Pharisees did not take prompt action against Jesus. Were they afraid of Him? Did He, after all, have a message from heaven, such as they had heard Him say, and was God really with Him? With absorbing interest they watched the outcome of the encounter.

"Esaias prophesied of you hypocrites." Never after this would either the people or the Pharisees read Isaiah but they would recall the words of Jesus. The Pharisees had intended to humiliate Jesus. He had turned the tables on them. They said nothing. There was nothing to say.

But Jesus was not done. He had been challenged on the matter of tradition, and He would use the occasion to make known His stand. Addressing the people, He said, "In vain do they worship Me, teaching for doctrines the commandments of men." Verse 7.

Vain Worship

"In vain do they worship." We can think of nothing worse for a Christian than vain worship, useless worship, worship that does not count. A man may bow down before God; he may pray to Him and call upon His name; he may count himself as one who enjoys the favor of God; but it is all in vain, if he is "teaching for doctrines the commandments of men."

Jesus continued, "For laying aside the commandment of God, ye hold the tradition of men, as the washing of pots and cups: and many other such like things do ye. And He said unto them, Full well ye reject the commandment of God, that ye may keep your own tradition." Mark 7:8, 9.

In these words Jesus touched the crux of the question. Men reject the commandments of God, that they may keep the tradition of men. This is what constitutes vain worship. They were making the word of God of none effect through their tradition.

Jesus never answered the question why His disciples ate with unwashed hands. He could have done so, had He wished, but He considered the matter of washing of little importance in itself. What He did consider important was the larger question, that of tradition. This issue He connects with the commandments of God, and for this He strikes a hard blow—a hard blow *against* tradition, a hard blow *for* the commandments of God.

The fact that Jesus took a relatively unimportant question and made it the occasion of stating a principle, makes the issue and question a most important one. It was not to the washing as such that He objected; that was an innocent ceremony. But when a matter, however small, touched the commandments of God and made them of none effect, then Christ was interested. It was the commandments about which He was concerned.

Corban

To illustrate the point of setting aside the commandments of God in favor of tradition, Jesus chose the fifth commandment. The Jews had a reprehensible custom which served them as an excuse for not supporting their aged parents. It was the duty of children to provide for them, but many would let the parents shift for themselves or be supported by public charity.

This latter, however, could be done only in case the children were unable to support their parents. If the children had property or income, the duty of support devolved upon them, which was a just and equitable arrangement. There was a way, however, by which they could escape doing that which should have been to them not merely a duty but a privilege. A man could dedicate his property to the temple. He would not need to give the dedicated property to the temple immediately; he could retain it for his own use as long as he lived, and at his death it would revert to the temple. This custom was called "corban."

A man might never have thought of giving anything to the Lord, but if the authorities demanded that he support his parents, he could suddenly declare his property "corban." Now the government could not take it away from him—it was dedicated to the Lord. Since he did not have to deliver it to the temple immediately, he could use it as long as he lived. By the time of his death it might be used up or worn out, so that it was useless, and, also, his parents would probably be dead by that time.

Thus corban accomplished the following: It excused a man from supporting his parents: it gave him a reputation for liberality in giving to the Lord, since all his substance was dedicated to God; and it did this without depriving him of anything. He had really given nothing, and yet he received credit for having given all.

Against this hypocrisy Jesus protested.

"He said unto them, Full well ye reject the commandment of God, that ye may keep your own tradition. For Moses said, Honor thy father and thy mother; and, Whoso curseth father or mother, let him die the death: but ye say, If a man shall say to his father or mother, It is Corban, that is to say, a gift, by whatsoever thou mightest be profited by me; he shall be free. And ye suffer him no more to do aught for his father or his mother; making the word of God of none effect through your tradition, which ye have delivered: and many such like things do ye." Mark 7:9-13.

With Jesus, human considerations and the law of God outweighed tradition. While Jesus in this instance used the fifth commandment as an illustration, we are not to think that it was only in regard to this commandment that the Pharisees were making the word of God of no effect. Christ adds significantly, "and many such like things do ye." Verse 13. A study of the history of the Jews reveals that it was not one or two commandments only which they made of none effect through their tradition. Every one of the ten suffered. Christ's saying, "Many such like things do ye," is significant and revealing.

From a mere human viewpoint we can see little reason for Christ's making an issue of the matter of washing the hands. If ever there was an innocent tradition, this certainly was one. Christ might just as well have told His disciples, "The Pharisees are much concerned about washing the hands before eating. I have no faith in any mere ceremony as such, but I see nothing wrong about washing the hands. If it will please them and avoid offense, perhaps we had better all wash after this. At least no harm can come from it."

We repeat, Christ could have said this, and we would have agreed with Him. But Christ did not say this.

117

There was more involved than appeared on the surface, and Christ used this opportunity to inculcate the lesson He had in mind. Let the careful reader note that Christ could easily have avoided clashing with the Pharisees on this point. That He chose to bring the matter to an issue over this seemingly insignificant point shows that He had something in mind to teach that generation and succeeding ones. Christ was definitely attacking tradition. He was not evading the issue. He was seeking it. He had something to say in regard to tradition, and He said it.

"Many such like things do ye." That was true of them, and it is true of us. We do many things as a mere matter of tradition—innocent things, many of them, and some of them not so innocent. For as truly now as then, men lay aside the commandments of God to hold to their tradition.

Pharisees and the Sabbath

Perhaps the regulations of the Pharisees in regard to Sabbathkeeping will serve as well as any to illustrate how the law of God was hedged about with restrictions that did not have God's sanction. They were simply traditions venerable with age which the people believed to be part of the law of Moses, and of binding force on the conscience. The Pharisees knew better, but were willing that the people should believe as they did.

The Sabbathkeeping of the Pharisees was mostly negative, as indeed was much of their religion. They had many rules regarding what was forbidden on the Sabbath—regulations which made the Sabbath a day of gloom and depression. Few Jews in the time of Christ would ever think of giving a patient a drink of water on the Sabbath to relieve fever, or in fact of giving anyone in need a drink of cold water. If one took sick on the Sabbath, he would have to wait till the sun went down before he could expect any help. Their hypocrisy in this is shown in the fact that if an ox fell into a pit on the Sabbath, they would work all day to rescue the ox; on the other hand, they would not lift a finger to relieve a suffering human being. No wonder Christ called them hypocrites. Luke 13:15; 14:5.

Some of the sheep which the Jews kept had very heavy tails, tails so heavy that they weighed as much as the sheep themselves. Being heavy, the tail would drag on the ground, the wool would be worn off, the skin torn, and blood would flow. To relieve the sheep, light wooden boards were fastened to the tail. These boards would drag on the ground and preserve the tail from damage and bring relief to the sheep. However, on the Sabbath the boards would be removed; for it could not be permitted, of course, to let the sheep carry this burden on the Sabbath. It is doubtful that the sheep enjoyed the Sabbath very much.

Of a piece with this legislation was the prohibition against carrying so much as a thin rug to use for a bed. One story of this kind is recorded in John 5:5-16. A man was not permitted to use a crutch on the Sabbath, and if he had a wooden leg, it had to be removed.

While there was a rule in regard to how far a man might walk on the Sabbath, the Pharisees taught that if he should partake of food at the end of the prescribed journey, then that particular place where he ate could be considered his home, and he could travel another Sabbath day's journey from that place. This he could repeat when he again came to the end of the prescribed distance, and thus he could continue as far as he cared. There was one difficulty, however. To carry the food with him would in itself be a breach of the Sabbath; so that could not be done. Hence he must either on the previous day deposit the food where it would be wanted, or arrange with someone who lived near the designated place to give him something to eat; then the letter of the law would be fulfilled, and he could travel on.

With all such rules Christ had scant patience. With emphasis He declared that the Sabbath was made for man, and not man for the Sabbath. The Pharisees, however, were sure that if these safeguards of the Sabbath were broken down, the Sabbath itself would also go. When Christ brushed away the multitudinous rules with which the Sabbath had been encumbered, some thought that He was attacking the Sabbath institution itself. Nothing was farther from the mind of Christ. He revered, He kept, the Sabbath. But the many restrictions which the people thought Moses had commanded, Christ ignored or deliberately transgressed. He would free the Sabbath from all extraneous regulations which God had never commanded, and give His people the Sabbath as God originally intended it, a blessing to mankind and to all creation.

Has the Sabbath Been Changed?

THE Old Testament declares that the seventh day is the Sabbath of the Lord. In regard to this there is no difference of opinion among Bible students. God rested the seventh day, blessed and hallowed it, and commanded men to keep it holy. There is no repeal of the Sabbath or of any of the other commandments in the Old Testament. As far as we are aware, there is no dissent anywhere to the statement that the seventh day is the Sabbath of the Old Testament.

When we come to the New Testament there is a difference of opinion in regard to what it teaches with reference to the law and the Sabbath. A large number of church members observe the first day of the week instead of the seventh, and believe that they have grounds for this observance in the teaching and example of Christ and the apostles. It therefore becomes our duty to inquire what the New Testament teaches in regard to Sabbath observance.

As Christians we are vitally concerned with the teaching of Christ and the apostles. In the final analysis Christ is our example and guide in all Christian duties. Christ is the Saviour of all men, Jew and Gentile alike. There is no other name in heaven or in earth by which we are to be saved. While Christ lived in Judea, His message is not a Judean message. His love and salvation are all-embracing. To follow Him is life; to reject Him is death. He

121

came to this world that we might have an object lesson in applied Christianity. He came to be the way, the truth, and the life. If we follow Him, we will not go astray. We agree with all Christians that there is no higher authority than Christ's. His word is final on all matters of life and doctrine.

The Law in the New Testament

When we speak of the law in this chapter, we mean the ten commandments as proclaimed by God on Mt. Sinai. There were other laws in existence at the time of Christ, such as the Mosaic sacrificial law, which had to do with the temple and the sacrifices connected with it. These ceremonial and temple laws terminated when the temple service ceased to be of value at the death of Christ. All Christians believe that they were abolished and annulled in the great sacrifice on Calvary. Col. 2:14. It is not of these laws that we speak, but of the law of God contained in the ten precepts. This law we believe to be of as much force as ever, and binding upon Christians and upon all men in all ages. Matt. 5:17-19; Luke 16:17; Rom. 3:31. It is to this law that we are addressing ourselves.

We have already discussed Christ's attitude toward the law. He made it very plain that He had not come to destroy the law, but to fulfill and magnify it. Isa. 42:21; Matt. 5:17-19. The Jews and the Pharisees tried repeatedly to catch Him in word or deed about the law, but they were unable to do so. Early in His ministry He made His position clear. He taught that not one jot or tittle of the law should pass. He stood stiffly for the law, and made that known to all. "Which of you convinceth Me of sin?" He challenged. John 8:46. There was no answer. Christ believed in and kept the law. "I have kept My Father's commandments," Christ says, "and abide in His love." John 15:10. There can be no dispute concerning this.

The apostles took the same stand on the law as did Christ. That, of course, would be expected. Those who hold that Paul spoke or wrote against the law put Paul against Christ. Paul indeed ignored the ceremonial law and taught that circumcision was without value, but when it came to the law of God, he stood exactly where Christ stood. Note how indignantly Paul repels the charge that faith makes void the law. "Do we then make void the law through faith?" he exclaims. "God forbid: yea, we establish the law." Rom. 3:31. There were no stronger words of protest that Paul could find than those he used, "God forbid." The charge was so preposterous, so out of harmony with all that he taught and believed, that he bursts out in vehement protest at the very thought of it. "Am I accused of teaching that the law is made void through faith? God forbid that I should teach any such thing. It is the farthest from my thought. No, I do not believe that the law is void. Just the contrary is the case. I establish it." He was of the same opinion as was Christ when He said, "It is easier for heaven and earth to pass, than one tittle of the law to fail." Luke 16:17.

The idea that either Christ or the apostles would attempt to annul the law of God is so strange and amazing that we cannot believe that men who speak thus are aware of the implication of their words. Abolish the law! Abolish the ten commandments! We can conceive that the evil one might desire to have this done, but we cannot believe that either Christ or the apostles would have anything to do with such an undertaking; nor do we believe that those who advocate such doctrine have considered what it means to abolish the law. Let us list the substance of each of the ten commandments, and consider the result were they to be abolished.

The Ten Commandments as Abolished

1. "Thou shalt have no other gods before Me." Abolished.

2. "Thou shalt not make unto thee any graven image." Abolished.

3. "Thou shalt not take the name of the Lord thy God in vain." Abolished.

4. "Remember the Sabbath day, to keep it holy." Abolished.

5. "Honor thy father and thy mother." Abolished.

6. "Thou shalt not kill." Abolished.

7. "Thou shalt not commit adultery." Abolished.

8. "Thou shalt not steal." Abolished.

9. "Thou shalt not bear false witness." Abolished.

10. "Thou shalt not covet." Abolished.

We confess that we are perplexed that anyone can think that Christ or the disciples ever attempted to abolish these commandments. With Paul we say, "God forbid."

Consider these commandments. Can a Christian look at them and say that they are, or ought to be, abolished? Is the commandment, "Thou shalt not steal," abolished? Or the commandment, "Thou shalt not commit adultery"? or, "Thou shalt have no other gods before Me"? God forbid! Such teaching is from beneath and not from above. Let all Christians forever banish any such idea from the mind. God did not proclaim the law from heaven and announce severe penalties for its transgression, merely to abolish it later. God did not lay down rules for man's conduct, then send His Son to die because men transgressed those rules, and immediately afterward annul the very law that demanded the death of Christ. If the law were to be annulled, it should have been annulled *before* Christ died. This would have saved Him the agony and terror of the cross. To keep the law in force just long enough to exact the penalty of death, and then annul it, is making the cross of none effect and Christ's death a miscarriage of justice.

Look once more at the law. Must we not agree with Paul that "the law is holy, and the commandment holy, and just, and good"? Rom. 7:12. Why should that which is holy and just and good be abolished? It is folly to charge Paul with making void that of which he thinks so highly. Must not all also agree with Paul that "the law is spiritual," and that the trouble is with us who are "carnal, sold under sin"? Rom. 7:14. We are sure that no Christian can point to these commandments and believe that they are abolished, or wish or hope to have them so. Rather, he will "consent unto the law that it is good." Verse 16. And that which is good should not be abolished.

We again express our amazement that religious teachers can believe in the abolition of the law. What do they mean by it? Surely not that men are now at liberty to disregard the commandments of God, that men may steal, kill, and commit adultery with impunity. That cannot be their idea. But if not, what do they mean when they say that the law is abolished? They do not believe that any one commandment is annulled as such, and yet they believe that the whole law is abolished. In some perplexity we again ask, Just what do they mean?

We believe we know what some of them mean. They hold that the day of the Sabbath has been changed from Saturday to Sunday. This, of course, cannot be done without changing the law. It seems inconsistent to them to abolish one of the ten commandments and only one, and so they abolish all, and re-enact such as they think should remain, which in this case means all but the fourth. This they rewrite as they think it should read. They do not ever believe that *all* of the fourth commandment is annulled. They contend that only that part of the commandment is annulled which deals with a specific day.

125

They hold that the *Sabbath* has not been abolished, but that the *seventh day* has.

This position brings the controversy out into the open. It is a question between the seventh and the first day of the week. The claim is that the Sabbath has been transferred from the seventh to the first day of the week; that Christ did this in virtue of His being Lord of the Sabbath, or that the disciples made the change.

The Apostles and the Sabbath

Let us first consider the possibility of the apostles' changing the Sabbath from one day to another. We would, of course, question the right of any man, however great, to change the law of Jehovah. We would question that God ever commissioned any man to do it. We would want a very definite declaration to that effect before believing it. God Himself, upon Mt. Sinai, proclaimed the law, prescribed severe penalties for its transgression, and enforced the law throughout the subsequent history of the Jews. It was this same law which He made the basis of His covenant with Israel, promising them great reward upon condition of obedience. We do not believe that any man, however great, has any right or mandate to change God's commandments.

A law publicly announced cannot be secretly annulled. If a change in the law is desired, the change should be made by as great authority as the one who first enacted it, and the nature of the change should be made plain. If, as in this case, the observance of one day is to be discontinued and the observance of another day ordered, this change must be made plain beyond the possibility of misunderstanding. Also, if the new day is to be honored with the same reverence as the old, then its institution should be accompanied with the same or greater manifestation of respect and honor.

God Himself led the way in the observance of the seventh-day Sabbath. He Himself proclaimed it in flaming fire from the mount. He Himself wrote it in enduring stone. Millions of God's people were witnesses and heard the proclamation, and myriads of angels were there.

None of these conditions was present at the time when the first day of the week was supposed to have been instituted. Sunday came in unannounced, unheralded, unnoticed, in every way an anticlimax to the original institution and inauguration of the Sabbath of the Lord. If God had anything to do with the first day of the week, we must draw the conclusion that He wanted the change made in the most secret and inconspicuous way possible; for on that first Sunday *nobody knew that any change had been made, not even the disciples,* who some say are supposed to have made it! They were in as complete ignorance as the rest, having locked themselves in a room for fear of the Jews. John 20:19.

We can see no consistency in God's announcing a law from heaven in the presence of millions of beings from this world and the world beyond, a law that is to judge the living and the dead, announcing it with all the glory and majesty at His command, so that the very earth quakes and the mountains tremble, and then abolishing that same law in the most inconspicuous manner, letting men find out years later what He has done. One would almost come to the conclusion that God was ashamed of what He had done. At least we are clear that the disciples had nothing to do with it. They did not even know that Christ had risen.

If it be objected that it is not the Sabbath that is abolished, but only the *day* of the Sabbath, we again call attention to the fact that when God instituted the Sabbath it was the seventh day He blessed. In the Garden of Eden all the morning stars sang together and all the sons of God shouted for joy. On Mt. Sinai, all Israel were witnesses to its proclamation. If all God's people were assembled when the seventh day was announced, should not God call all His people together when He decides to honor another day above the one He Himself called "the holy of the Lord?" Should God do less for the first day of the week than He did for the seventh?

God did everything that He could do to magnify the seventh-day Sabbath. He honored it by keeping it Himself. He rested upon it, He blessed it, He sanctified it, He proclaimed it in glory from the mount. He did none of these things for the first day of the week.

If God had determined to show the difference between the first and the seventh day of the week, if He had decided to show that the seventh day *is* the Sabbath and that the first day *is not,* He could do no better than point to the institution of the blessed, sanctified seventh day in splendor and glory at Mt. Sinai and in the Garden of Eden, and by way of contrast, unhallowed, unblessed Sunday, instituted in obscurity, arriving unannounced, unnoticed, unknown, even to the most intimate followers of Christ, who at the time were hiding behind bolted doors for fear of the Jews. This contrast alone is sufficient to show God's estimation of the two days.

Did God or Christ Change the Sabbath?

Christ had nothing to do with any change of the Sabbath day from the seventh to the first day of the week. If He had, He would never have done it in the way its advocates say it was done. According to their view, instead of heralding to the world the inauguration of a new rule of conduct, telling all that the old Sabbath had been abolished and that a new day had dawned, a glorious day, far surpassing in splendor the seventh-day Sabbath, its own advocates admit that Christ said nothing to anybody concerning it, and that His own disciples were completely in the dark. We submit that this is altogether unlike Christ. We know what God did in announcing the seventh-day Sabbath. Ought He not at least to have notified the disciples most concerned, so that they would not be in ignorance years after the event took place?

The whole conception seems entirely unlike God. If we are to have a new Sabbath, let the old one be abolished by divine fiat, and let the new one be honorably installed with at least as much respect paid to it as was paid the old. Let this be done as openly and publicly as when the Sabbath was first commanded and announced. Anything less than this would be to the detriment of the new day, would, in fact, place it under suspicion, and would reflect on God Himself.

In view of the fact that God has announced to the world and to angels that "the seventh day is the Sabbath of the Lord," that is, that it is God's own Sabbath; in view of the further fact that God has announced Himself as "the Lord, I change not;" in view of the still further fact that He is "the Father of lights, with whom is no variableness, neither shadow of turning," would it not be embarrassing to Him to announce that a change had been made in the day of the Sabbath; that the seventh day which He had pronounced holy was no longer holy; that henceforth it was not to be known as "My holy day," "the holy of the Lord, honorable;" that another day had been chosen in its stead; that He had removed the blessing and sanctification with which He had once invested the Sabbath; that it was now demoted to a common working day; and that while men had formerly been punished for profaning the Sabbath, they could now work all they wanted to on the seventh day, and be guiltless? Mal. 3:6; James 1:17; Isa. 58:13. How could God after such an announcement ever claim to be the One who changeth not, the "Father of lights, with whom there is no variableness" or "shadow of turning"?

God and Angels

But if it would be embarrassing for God to make such an announcement to men, would it not be equally or even more embarrassing to make it to angels? They were present at the time of the giving of the law on Sinai. They were present in the Garden of Eden when God rested on that first beautiful Sabbath. They were present when the man in the wilderness went out to gather sticks on the Sabbath, and they saw what happened to him. But now for some reason God has changed. The angels are in perplexity. They have associated and worked with men since the days of creation. They have patiently helped and instructed them; they have warned them not to profane the Sabbath; they have assisted conscience in bringing men back to a realization of their errors; they have been used by the Spirit in convincing men of sin; and again and again they have instructed men in the sacredness of God's holy day. Even the week before the supposed change of the Sabbath took place, they were engaged in teaching men the sacredness of God's holy Sabbath. But now the following week a change has come. The Sabbath is no longer the Sabbath. They will now have to educate men's conscience over again; and they wonder how they will justify God in the sight of men, how they will justify the law. To them this is no small matter. They are perplexed, and do not feel free to go to God for help. Something has happened to God. He has changed, despite the fact that He claims that He never changes.

Angels, of course, did not reason thus, for God would never put Himself in a position that would call for such reasoning. Whatever God does, He does openly and above board. If He had thought best to introduce another day than the Sabbath, He would have been as open about it as He was in the introduction of the seventh-day Sabbath.

He would not secretly, surreptitiously, almost ashamedly, institute a new, and as its defenders say, a far more glorious day than the first Sabbath. No, a thousand times no! Such a day would deserve a better introduction, as much greater and more glorious as the first day of the week is supposed to be greater and more glorious than the seventh! As God once spoke from heaven telling men their duty, so He would again speak if He changed His requirements. This would seem the only fair way, and would meet the approbation of mankind.

If there was any justification for God's coming down on Mt. Sinai to announce to men the ten commandments, there is the same justification for God's coming down the second time should He wish to change His law. God with His own voice spoke the law and commanded men to keep it. God actually wrote the ten commandments on two tables of stone and gave them to men, that they might know exactly what He said. Men have a right to expect God to stand by His word. In all fairness, if God wants to change the rules of life, He should ask for the return of the two tables of stone; He should clearly and definitely state the new commandments which men were henceforth to observe; and, if a change of the Sabbath day was in contemplation, He should give the reasons for such a change as He originally gave reasons for keeping the seventh-day Sabbath. He should, for His own sake, make some explanation why He once asked men to "remember the Sabbath day, to keep it holy," and now asks them to forget it. In justice to Himself He should make this clear, that men might not err. The only pronouncement which men have so far is God's words from Sinai. Men have a right to expect God to stand by this pronouncement until such time as He openly repudiates the old and announces the new conditions of life. Men's sense of fairness demands this; God's demands much more.

Christ Lord of the Sabbath

When Christ proclaimed Himself Lord of the Sabbath, did this mean that He had a right to change the Sabbath day, and that He did so? Let us consider this.

The Pharisees presumed to make rules for the observance of the Sabbath—rules which God did not countenance—and complained to Christ that His disciples did not observe them. This was the occasion for Christ's saying that He is Lord of the Sabbath. Just what did He mean by this?

When Christ claimed Lordship over the Sabbath, He in effect said, "I am the One to make the rules, not you. I am Lord of the Sabbath." This statement, made under such circumstances, would forever debar the Pharisees, the disciples, or any others from making any claim that they had any right over the Sabbath. Christ alone has that. He is Lord of the Sabbath. This would, of course, have direct application to such as felt themselves capable of changing or abrogating the Sabbath commandment. In just so many words Christ tells them that the Sabbath is under His jurisdiction, and that they have no control over it whatsoever. He has given the Sabbath to man, but He wants man to know that He is Lord of it.

We have noted elsewhere that it was Christ who in the beginning made the Sabbath. This is clear from such passages as John 1:3: "All things were made by Him; and without Him was not anything made that was made." Among the things that were made, "the Sabbath was made." Mark 2:27. It is therefore clear that Christ made the Sabbath.

In view of this, Christ's statement that He is Lord of the Sabbath takes on new meaning. Christ is Lord of all, and He is Lord *also* of the Sabbath. The word "also" in this connection is significant. There are those who are willing to accept Christ as Lord of many things, but not as Lord of the Sabbath. But to deny His Lordship in one thing is to deny it in all. Christians who accept Christ as their Lord should also accept Him as Lord of the Sabbath. If they do this, they will accept Him as Lord of the seventh-day Sabbath, for that was the day observed when Christ proclaimed Himself Lord of it. The Sabbath was then a "going concern." Christ would not be eager to proclaim Himself Lord of that which was about to be abolished.

If Christ was and is Lord of the Sabbath, we understand better His attitude toward it while He was among men. We can but believe that Christ even on earth was fully aware of the prominence given to the Sabbath in the Old Testament; how it was a test and a sign, and how men had been punished for willfully profaning it. He could not but be fully aware of the fact that for centuries God had tried to teach Israel the importance of the Sabbath, but that they had ignored His prophets and teachers. Now at last they had had their eyes opened to its importance, and had begun to esteem it highly as one of God's choicest gifts. But, alas, the evil one had pushed them to the other extreme, and the Pharisees had completely destroyed the beauty and meaning of the Sabbath by imposing un-Biblical regulations upon its observance.

We believe that Christ knew all this, and also about the future; He was acquainted with the fact that Sunday would be introduced into the church as the successor of the Sabbath, and that He and His disciples would be accused of having changed the day.

In view of this foreknowledge, it would seem to us that when Christ spoke of the law or the Sabbath, He would be very careful to so weigh and measure His words and His acts that there could remain no doubt in the mind of any regarding what He meant. Knowing that Christ knew the future and the controversy that would rage about the Sabbath, we would reverently ask Him a few questions and acquaint Him with some things that we wish might be done. Here are some things we would like to know.

Some Questions

1. We would like to have Christ make very clear whether the law proclaimed on Mt. Sinai is still in force, or whether it has been abrogated or changed in any manner whatsoever. We are anxious about this, and would like an unequivocal statement about the law. It is clear, of course, that if the law from Sinai is still in force, if it has not been annulled or changed, then "the seventh day is the Sabbath of the Lord thy God." We would like to have a statement from Christ's own mouth in regard to whether He considers this law still in effect. Has the law been changed in any way? Has so much as a jot or tittle been changed? We reverently ask this question of the Master, and hope that He will answer it; for some great men say that the law has been changed, while others say that it has not. Christ is the only one who can settle the question. We sincerely hope and pray that He will do so.

2. We would like to know whether any man has a right to change the law or the Sabbath. We would like to know whether a *great* man has a right to do this. In view of the fact that the Papacy claims the right to make such a change, we would like to know whether this claim was known to God beforehand; and if it were, and if God knew of all the confusion that such a claim would make—that millions would believe it—we would humbly inquire if it would not have been a good thing for God to expose such a diabolical plan beforehand and unmask the deceiver, so that all men might know that God had nothing to do with such a dastardly undertaking. We would not presume to dictate to God, but if God knew of all this, we would think

it fitting for God to reveal the plot, so that all men might know the truth. So we reverently ask, first, whether God knew of this, and, second, what precautions He took, if any. We are simple-minded enough to believe that the answer would be helpful to mankind.

3. We would like to know whether God knew beforehand of the millions who would desert the Sabbath of the Lord and keep the first day of the week instead; and if He did, what steps, if any, He took to inform the world that Sunday is not the Sabbath of the Lord, but just an ordinary working day. We would like not merely to know that the seventh day *is* the Sabbath of the Lord; we would also like to have Him say that the first day is *not* the Sabbath. We would like to have God place the two days side by side, and say, This day *is* the Sabbath, and this day is *not* the Sabbath. We would not dictate to God—we repeat this— but in our heart of hearts we wish that God would make the matter very plain.

4. We wish that God would do one more thing. The Bible says that the Sabbath is a sign of sanctification, but it seems to us that the world has not had a very convincing demonstration of that. True, the Jews observed the seventh day, but they have not always been a good example of the sanctifying power of God. We wish that God would make another demonstration. We wish that He would select a people, just a common, ordinary people, and make them an object lesson to the world of what He can do with lowly clay; we wish that He would give them the Sabbath as of old, that He would sanctify them wholly, and then make some such demonstration as was made on Mt. Carmel when Elijah stood alone against the false prophets of Baal and Astarte. We wish that He would send another Elijah before the great and terrible day of the Lord, and give men a chance to choose whom they will serve, having all the facts before them. It seems to us that the claims of

Sabbath and Sunday should be made clear to all, and that the knowledge of God and His Sabbath should be spread like the leaves of autumn. We would like to see the earth be lighted with the knowledge of God, that all men might know what their duty is. In other words, we would like to see the question of Sabbath and Sunday come to the front among the questions of the day, the merits of the two days be freely discussed, and all the world know that there is a controversy going on. We would like to see the work of God finished in a blaze of glory and not be confined to a small and humble sect. We wish God would do something of the kind. To our minds He owes it to Himself to do this.

We have here asked a good many things of God. We hope that we have not been presumptuous in doing so. We might indeed confide to the reader that the questions here asked, God has already anticipated and answered, and many more. We would never have dared ask them, had we not known that God had the answer ready. He knew that such questions would come up in the mind, and He graciously provided the solution. Of this we shall now study.

Sunday in the New Testament

In the preceding chapter we expressed the wish that God would make the question of Sabbath and Sunday clear beyond possibility of misunderstanding. We expressed the hope that God would place the two days side by side in the New Testament, and say, This day *is* the Sabbath, and this day is *not* the Sabbath. Then all doubts would be forever resolved, and all uncertainties cleared away.

We are glad to know that God has done this very thing. Sabbath and Sunday are both mentioned in the New Testament; they are placed side by side in just the way we should like to see it done, and the two days are contrasted. That gives a fair opportunity for evaluating each of them, and to draw such conclusions as seem warranted from the evidence adduced.

Some have thought that it would have been better if only Sunday had been mentioned in the New Testament, and nothing said of the Sabbath. Others think that it would have been better if the Sabbath only had been made prominent and nothing whatever said of Sunday. Tuesday is not mentioned; why should Sunday be? If God did not want men to keep the first day of the week, why are there eight distinct references made to it in the New Testament? Does not that make for confusion and lend color to the contention that Sunday has some definite place in New Testament religion?

This argument will carry weight unless it can be shown

that God placed Sunday in the New Testament for the specific purpose of telling men that Sunday is not the Sabbath. This, we believe, is the very thing God has done.

As stated above, the first day of the week is mentioned eight times in the New Testament, but at no time is it called the Sabbath. The eight texts are found in the following places: Matthew 28:1; Mark 16:1, 2; Mark 16:9; Luke 24:1; John 20:1; John 20:19; Acts 20:7; 1 Corinthians 16:2.

The First Text

Acts 20:7 records the only religious meeting in the New Testament that was held on the first day of the week; so we shall consider it first. This is the reading of the text:

"Upon the first day of the week, when the disciples came together to break bread, Paul preached unto them, ready to depart on the morrow; and continued his speech until midnight."

Here a definitely religious meeting is recorded. It was held upon "the first day of the week, when the disciples came together to break bread." Paul was leaving "on the morrow" on a long journey. We are informed that he "continued his speech until midnight." A young man was sitting in a window, and "as Paul was long preaching, he sunk down with sleep, and fell down from the third loft, and was taken up dead." Verse 9. Paul, however, restored him to life, bread was broken, and Paul continued to speak "even till break of day." Then he took his departure, and went on foot a distance of about eighteen miles to meet the ship which was to take him on his way.

There are several questions that confront us in this account. First, When was the meeting held? The record shows that it was held in the evening, for there "were many lights in the upper chamber," and Paul spoke till midnight, and then continued "till break of day." The question is whether the meeting was held on Saturday or Sunday evening. As is known, the Bible reckons the day from sunset till sunset, while the common present reckoning is from midnight to midnight. When the Bible speaks of the first day of the week, the time from sunset Saturday till sunset Sunday is meant. Ordinarily a meeting held in the evening of the first day of the week would mean that it was held Saturday night; but there are indications that it was not always so reckoned, and hence it may be that this particular meeting was held on what we call Sunday night.

In the particular case under consideration, commentators are nearly evenly divided, some holding that the meeting occurred Saturday night, others, Sunday night. We have no special light on the question. We are willing to accept either view, as for our purpose it makes little difference. We leave this question for the reader to decide for himself according as he sees best. In any event a meeting was held, either Saturday or Sunday night. At that meeting Paul preached and bread was broken.

Was this a special meeting called because Paul was about to leave on a long journey, and this was the last opportunity he would have to meet with them before the boat sailed? The evidence seems to be in favor of this. It was unusual in those days to hold meetings at night, except in times of persecution, for it was dangerous to be abroad in the dark. Then, too, the gates of the city were closed at sunset, and no one who lived outside the city could conveniently attend such a meeting. We are therefore inclined to believe that this was an unusual meeting.

This is the only record in the New Testament of the disciples' meeting the first day of the week to break bread. Acts 2:46 states that they contiuued "daily with one accord in the temple, and breaking bread from house to house." This states that they broke bread daily, which would, of course, include the first day of the week; but there is no record that bread was broken only on that day, to the exclusion of other days.

The question in which we are interested is that of whether this meeting on the first day of the week proves that this day was the Sabbath; that is, whether the disciples were observing the first day of the week as the Sabbath at this time, and whether Paul was observing the first day with them, meeting with them, speaking to them, and breaking bread with them? This is an important question that deserves study.

It is to be noted that the account of the meeting says nothing about the Sabbath. It would have been easy for Luke to insert a word, stating that this meeting was held on the Sabbath. That he does not do this is significant. It seems clear that the reason for the meeting's being recorded in the Bible is the fact that a miracle was performed. A dead man was brought back to life again, and Luke notes this unusual happening. It was not often that such an event took place, and Luke recorded it.

The other events of the meeting are mentioned incidentally, and apparently were not of chief concern. We are not, for instance, told the subject of Paul's talk. We know, therefore, that it was not the sermon that impelled Luke to report the meeting. If the meeting had anything to do with the observance of the first day of the week, we may be sure that Luke would have reported this most important fact. Also the fact that nothing is said of Paul's speech, is proof that it did not deal with the subject of a new Sabbath. All that Luke says about the speech is that Paul "continued his speech until midnight," "was long preaching," "talked a long while, even till break of day." Luke was not greatly impressed with the content of the sermon.

There are other questions that call for consideration. If the meeting was held Saturday night—which to many seems most likely—then Paul had a long journey ahead of him for Sunday. Would Paul have undertaken such a journey on the new Sabbath? Luke, who is the author of the book of Acts, as well as of the third Gospel, in reporting the events of the crucifixion and resurrection of Christ, makes note of the fact that the women did not attempt to embalm the body on the Sabbath, but "rested the Sabbath day," and that this resting was "according to the commandment." The time of the writing of the book of Luke and that of Acts is not far apart. Is it conceivable that he would not faithfully make a record of such a drastic change as that from Saturday to Sunday, had such a change occurred? If this particular meeting took place on Saturday night, Paul started his journey of eighteen miles at daybreak to get to his boat. This would hardly be an auspicious introduction of the first-day Sabbath, either to the church there or to New Testament readers.

If, on the other hand, this meeting was held Sunday night, then it was not held on the first day of the week at all, for the first day ended at sunset Sunday evening, and this meeting was held later than sunset. Should we even admit of midnight as the beginning of the new day according to our present reckoning, we would still be in difficulty, for the meeting lasted till Monday morning, and the bread was broken after midnight. We confess that the record seems to us quite unsatisfactory if it is to be used as a prop for Sundaykeeping.

From the record of the meeting we learn the following:

The meeting was a special meeting, held because Paul was about to leave on a journey and wanted to break bread with the church once more before they parted.

The meeting was reported by Luke because of the restoration of the young man who fell down and was killed.

There was no great theological or other issue at stake, and Paul's sermon has not been preserved for us, which it would have been had it been of unusual importance.

This last consideration would rule out that the meeting or sermon had anything to do with the Sabbath question. Luke, who was a faithful historian and had a "perfect understanding of all things from the very first," would be quick to detect any variation from the usual procedure. Luke 1:3.

While the first day is mentioned in this account, nothing is said of its being the Sabbath. This night meeting, if it had any relation whatever to the Sabbath question, would have presented an excellent opportunity for the historian, Luke, to record any new development in the teaching since the days of Christ. The fact that he records a meeting held on the first day of the week, coupled with the fact that he conspicuously omits any mention of it as a Sabbath meeting held in honor of Sunday, is conclusive proof that he did not consider it to have any relation to the Sabbath whatsoever. We believe that inspiration purposely recorded a meeting as being held on the first day of the week to give opportunity for the observant reader to note that God does not recognize the first day as the Sabbath.

If the holding of a meeting on the first day of the week is proof of that day's being the Sabbath, or that it has any bearing on the Sabbath question, what shall we say of the meeting which Paul held in Antioch on the seventh-day Sabbath? Acts 13:14. That would balance the argument, for now we have the record of one meeting held on the Sabbath and one on Sunday. But Paul held a meeting the next Sabbath also! Verse 44. That would make the argument twice as strong for the Sabbath as for Sunday! But that is not all. In Thessalonica he held meetings on three Sabbaths. Acts 17:2. That makes the argument five to one in favor of the Sabbath. But even that is not all. At Corinth he stayed "a year and six months," and "he reasoned in the synagogue every Sabbath, and persuaded the Jews and the Greeks." Acts 18:11, 4. A year and six months are seventy-eight weeks and the same number of Sabbaths. Added to the previously recorded five Sabbaths, this makes a total of eighty-three recorded meetings that Paul held on the Sabbath, and the ratio is now eighty-three to one in favor of the Sabbath as against Sunday.

We, however, reject any such reasoning. The number of times meetings are held on a certain day has no bearing whatever on the question of that day's being the Sabbath. But to any who believe that the fact that Acts records a meeting as being held on Sunday has any bearing on the question of that day's being the Sabbath, we submit the above computation.

We have now examined the only text in the New Testament that records any religious meeting held on the first day of the week. We have found nothing that even remotely connects it with the Sabbath. There is no mention of it as a holy day or of any observance of it. We now turn to the consideration of the second text.

The Second Text

This text is recorded in 1 Corinthians 16:1, 2. "Now concerning the collection for the saints, as I have given order to the churches of Galatia, even so do ye. Upon the first day of the week let every one of you lay by him in store, as God hath prospered him, that there be no gatherings when I come."

Paul here exhorts the saints to lay by on the first day of the week a sum proportionate to the prospering hand of God. He had ordered the same to be done in the other churches in Galatia.

Some have thought that this refers to a collection to be

taken in the churches on Sunday, and that Paul was giving directions in regard to how it should be done. It is to be noted, however, that neither church nor meeting is mentioned. Each man was to lay "by him in store." "By him" means "by himself," or "at home," as it is also translated. "In store" means that he should keep it until it was called for.

Paul knew the value of systematic giving. He was making a collection for the poor saints, and he knew that unless the people laid by a little every week, there would not be much for him to collect when the time came.

How much was each to give? Paul did not say; but he suggested that he give "as God hath prospered" him, which was a reasonable way of giving. This is the same principle that governs tithe paying, with which all Israel was familiar. The man who earned much would give correspondingly, while he who earned little would give according to his income.

This God-ordained plan is most equitable. It of course necessitates some system of keeping a record of the income, especially in the case of businessmen; for if they are to give weekly, they must look over their accounts weekly, or they would be unable to know how God had prospered them. Paul recommended that this work be done on Sunday.

These people were doubtless familiar with the principle already; so all they needed was a reminder. The suggestion that the examination of the accounts be done on the first day of the week might have been new to them, but the principle of proportionate giving was not new. Paul might have thought that some of them would be tempted to do this examining of accounts on the Sabbath, and so he suggests that it be done on the first day of the week. At that time they were to go over the record, and as God had prospered them they were to lay by in store.

Those who use this advice of Paul's as an argument for Sunday sacredness—a most curious use indeed—make several mistakes.

They fail to note that this is not a public collection.

They fail to note that this is not speaking of a church service.

They fail to note that this money is not to be given in a collection to be taken then and there, but is to be kept "in store" until such time as it is called for.

They fail to note that this setting aside of funds is to be done "by him," that is by each person, at home, not in church, not in company, but by himself.

They fail to note that the gift of each is to be proportionate to the prosperity with which God has blessed him, and that this calls for a weekly accounting, to determine the income, and a weekly laying aside according to the amount of income. This might in some cases involve considerable bookkeeping, which would be altogether inappropriate to do on the Sabbath, but which Paul considers to be good work on Sunday.

A careful reading of Paul's advice in the text before us results in the conviction that the text constitutes a sound argument for the sacredness of the seventh-day Sabbath, and a strong argument against Sunday sacredness.

We now turn to a consideration of the six remaining texts, all of which deal with the day of the resurrection.

The Third Text

This text is found in Matthew 28:1: "In the end of the Sabbath, as it began to dawn toward the first day of the week, came Mary Magdalene and the other Mary to see the sepulcher." The Revised Version reads, "Now late on the Sabbath day, as it began to dawn toward the first day of the week, came Mary Magdalene and the other Mary to see the sepulcher."

10   145

There are differences of opinion among translators in regard to the correct rendering of this text, but for our present purpose we are willing to accept either of the translations given above. The text mentions two days. The one is called the Sabbath; the other is called the first day of the week. The Sabbath comes before the first day, and is definitely distinguished from it. There is no intermingling or confusion of days, and no change of the Sabbath day is suggested. We are simply informed that in the end of the Sabbath, as it began to dawn toward the first day of the week, Mary Magdalene and the other Mary came to the sepulcher.

It is interesting to note what this text says, and also what it does not say. The Gospel of Matthew was written about thirty years after the death of Christ. In that time the Holy Spirit had ample time to impress upon the hearts of the leading disciples that a new Sabbath had come into existence, if that indeed were the case. It would be most fitting if some reference to this supposed fact had been made when Matthew mentions the resurrection. It would have been easy to make some remark that would indicate that the old Sabbath was superseded by the new. It seems passing strange that thirty years after the resurrection, Matthew still calls the seventh day the Sabbath, and fails to improve the opportunity of putting in a word for Sunday.

Inspiration, of course, foresaw that there would be a controversy about the two days. That controversy could have been settled in the text before us, if Matthew had only stated that the new Sabbath had taken the place of the old. As he did not do this, may we not believe that he settled the controversy by calling the seventh day the Sabbath and completely neglecting to recognize or make any claim for Sunday as the Sabbath?

The Fourth and Fifth Texts

The fourth text reads as follows: "When the Sabbath was past, Mary Magdalene, and Mary the mother of James, and Salome, had bought sweet spices, that they might come and anoint Him. And very early in the morning the first day of the week, they came unto the sepulcher at the rising of the sun." Mark 16:1, 2. To this we would add the fifth text, found in the same chapter. "Now when Jesus was risen early the first day of the week, He appeared first to Mary Magdalene, out of whom He had cast seven devils." Mark 16:9.

Verse 9 refers to the same first day mentioned in verse two. It states that Jesus first appeared to Mary Magdalene when He arose early the first day of the week. It does not state that the first day of the week is the Sabbath; it merely affirms that on that day Christ met Mary Magdalene.

Verse 2 states that the women mentioned in verse 1 came to the sepulcher on the first day of the week as the sun was rising. We are told that they came to anoint the Saviour, and brought sweet spices with them for that purpose. The statement is also made that "the Sabbath was past" when they started on their errand.

Here again we have the two days placed side by side, the Sabbath and the first day of the week. We are told that the Sabbath is the day that precedes the first day of the week, and that when the first day comes, the Sabbath is past. We again note that inspiration, speaking through Mark as it had through Matthew, thirty years after the resurrection, calls the seventh day the Sabbath, and that the only name given Sunday is the first day of the week.

We would again suggest that it would have been easy for the inspired writer to put in a word for Sunday in this particular place. That he failed to do so is significant.

147

We would further suggest that, if the inspired writer did not wish to exalt Sunday, he might have remained neutral or silent on the question. But he does not. He tells us that the day before Sunday, that is, the seventh day, is the Sabbath. *That* is putting in a good word for the Sabbath. But he does more than that. He tells us that the women did work on Sunday which they would not do on the Sabbath, important as that work was. This is more than neutrality. It is definite bias in favor of the Sabbath as against Sunday. Note carefully the situation.

Christ died on Friday. On that day the women bought spices and prepared them, ready to embalm the body. Luke 23:56. When the Sabbath was past, they came to the sepulcher early at the rising of the sun to begin their work. That is, they worked Friday and Sunday, but not on the Sabbath. These were the women who were nearest Christ, His closest followers. Of them inspiration reports, thirty years after the death of Christ, that they did not work on the Sabbath, but that they did work on Sunday. The text does not enlarge on this; it merely refers to it as a matter of fact.

It was necessary to embalm bodies as soon as possible in a climate such as that of Palestine. Of Lazarus it is stated that his body on the fourth day "stinketh," in the expressive though somewhat inelegant language of the time of King James. John 11:39. Sunday was the third day since Christ's death, as then reckoned. If there ever was any excuse for working on the Sabbath, it would seem that this would be the time. But the women had been with Christ. They had learned of Him. They knew how He kept the Sabbath. It never occurred to them to embalm His body on that day, and this despite the fact that the climate almost demanded it. Inspiration records that they waited till Sunday to do this work.

This text definitely contrasts Sabbath and Sunday. It

says in effect: "Do not work on the Sabbath. Keep that day holy. Do your work on the other days. However necessary it may seem to work on the Sabbath, do not do it. The God who preserved the manna, so that it did not spoil, can easily preserve a body from corruption. Remember the Sabbath day, to keep it holy."

The Sixth Text

The sixth text is found in Luke 24:1. "Now upon the first day of the week, very early in the morning, they came unto the sepulcher, bringing the spices which they had prepared, and certain others with them."

This is the same event which the other evangelists record, with some added information. The preceding verses read: "That day was the preparation, and the Sabbath drew on. And the women also, which came with Him from Galilee, followed after, and beheld the sepulcher, and how His body was laid. And they returned, and prepared spices and ointments; and rested the Sabbath day according to the commandment." Luke 23:54-56.

We learn from this that on the day of preparation, that is, Friday, Christ was crucified, and that He died as the Sabbath was drawing on. We learn also that the women that same Friday prepared spices for His anointing, and that on the following day, Saturday, they rested "according to the commandment." If we take these verses in connection with Luke 24:1, we find that three days are under review, the day of preparation, the Sabbath, and the first day of the week. We are told that the women worked two of these days, but that on the Sabbath they rested.

There is nothing in these texts that says or suggests that Sunday is the Sabbath. On the contrary, the difference between Sunday and the Sabbath is made very distinct and clear. The women worked on the day of preparation, Friday. On Saturday they did not work; they rested, and this was "according to the commandment." On Sunday they brought their material to anoint their Lord. This makes a definite contrast between the two days, and makes emphatic that the day which comes between Friday and Sunday is "the Sabbath day according to the commandment." This, then, makes Saturday the Sabbath of the Lord. Nothing is said of Sunday sacredness. The only mention is that on Sunday the women came carrying the material, ready to go to work.

We would call special attention to one word that takes on some importance, the word "now," the first word in the statement, "Now upon the first day of the week." Luke 24:1. The word in the original is "but," not "now." The Revised Version correctly reads, "But on the first day of the week." If we read the context, we are made aware of the contrast which the word "but" is meant to convey. The women "rested the Sabbath day according to the commandment, *but* upon the first day of the week, . . . " The contrast here is between the Sabbath and the first day of the week. On the Sabbath they rested, *but*. The statement is clear, and so is the meaning; they rested on the Sabbath, *but* on the first day they worked. The "but" should be given all the weight which inspiration has put in it.

This text states definitely which day *is* the Sabbath in the New Testament, and also which day *is not* the Sabbath. It states which day is "the Sabbath day according to the commandment," states that the women who followed Christ rested on that day, but that on the next day they did not rest. We have, therefore, here an inspired statement that the day before Sunday is "the Sabbath day according to the commandment," and that hence Sunday cannot be the Sabbath; and we have an inspired "but" to show the contrast between the two days. It is the same "but" that is in the commandment itself with the same contrast, though reversed, "Six days shalt thou labor, and do all thy work:

but the seventh day is the Sabbath of the Lord thy God."
Ex. 20:9, 10.

The Seventh and Eighth Texts

These two texts are found in John 20:1, 19. "The first
day of the week cometh Mary Magdalene early, when it
was yet dark, unto the sepulcher, and seeth the stone taken
away from the sepulcher." "Then the same day at evening, being the first day of the week, when the doors were
shut where the disciples were assembled for fear of the
Jews, came Jesus and stood in the midst, and saith unto
them, Peace be unto you."

The first of these texts repeats what the other evangelists
have said, and appears to add nothing new or different.
The first day is mentioned, but nothing is said of its being
the Sabbath. It merely records that Mary Magdalene
came early the first day of the week to the grave, which
same statement is made by the other evangelists.

The second text mentions that the disciples were assembled that "same day at evening, being the first day of the
week," that is, Sunday evening. We are not told the purpose of their assembly. The doors were shut, bolted, "for
fear of the Jews."

At this time the disciples were in ignorance of the
resurrection of Jesus. Because of this ignorance we know
that they were not assembled to celebrate the resurrection.
Though they knew that Christ was not in the tomb, they
simply could not believe that He was risen from the dead.
We also know that they were not assembled to celebrate a
new Sabbath in commemoration of the resurrection, for
the reason just stated, that they did not believe that Christ
had risen. All we know is that they were together, and
that they were afraid of the Jews and had bolted the doors.

It is not easy to understand how any can see in this

151

account an argument for Sunday sacredness. But inspiration knew that the time would come when men would grasp at any straw to support them in their contention for a first-day Sabbath. As a matter of historical accuracy, it was necessary to make a report of the meeting, for it was an important one, and inspiration must report the truth. But in this case inspiration took special precaution that there be no misunderstanding. God knew that the statement that the disciples were assembled Sunday night would be interpreted by some to mean that it was a religious meeting to celebrate the resurrection, or Sunday, or something. So inspiration makes it plain that the disciples were not meeting to celebrate the resurrection, or to celebrate Sunday. They were gathered for fear of the Jews, and not for the celebration of anything.

It might in passing be noted that while this meeting was held Sunday night, it was in reality not held on the *first,* but on the *second,* day of the week, for the first day, according to Biblical reckoning, closed with sunset Sunday evening. The first day of the week is not entirely synchronous with Sunday, for the civil day begins and ends at midnight, while the Biblical day begins and ends at sunset. The disciples were gathered on what we call Sunday night; but when Sunday night comes, the first day of the week is already ended, and the second day of the week is begun. According to the Biblical method of counting time, the meeting was held on the second day of the week and not on the first. However, as all are agreed that it was held on Sunday evening, we are not stressing this technical point. Either way, inspiration wants us to know that the disciples were not gathered to celebrate the first day of the week as Sabbath. But it is interesting to know that, technically speaking, there was no meeting at all held on the first day of the week.

Summary

We have now considered every text in the New Testament that mentions the first day of the week. Instead of finding them favorable to the first day of the week as the Sabbath, we find in them strong proof for the seventh-day Sabbath. We sum up the teaching of inspiration as follows:

When inspiration finds it necessary to mention the first day, it takes pains to contrast that day with the Sabbath. Inspiration could have used these opportunities to tell us that the first day henceforth was to be the Sabbath. It does not do so.

Inspiration could have mentioned the first day of the week without bringing it into contrast with the Sabbath. But it purposely makes the contrast prominent.

Inspiration could have referred to the seventh day without calling it the Sabbath. It might have called it the day preceding the first day of the week, thus avoiding calling it the Sabbath and at the same time making Sunday prominent. But it does nothing of the kind.

Inspiration could have avoided stating that the day that comes between Friday and Sunday is the Sabbath according to the commandment, but it does not try to avoid it. It makes that point prominent.

Inspiration could have avoided making as sharp a contrast as it does between Sabbath and Sunday by omitting the "but" in Luke 24:1. But inspiration seems determined to emphasize that point.

Inspiration could have recorded the meeting Sunday night without mentioning that the disciples had bolted the doors for fear of the Jews. Had that been omitted, the impression might have been left that it was some kind of celebration meeting. As it is now, we are told that they did not have any faith in the resurrection, and that, of course, spoils any idea of using this text in favor of Sunday sacredness.

We hold, therefore, that the references to the first day of the week in the New Testament have been put there by God Himself for the specific purpose of affirming that the seventh day *is* the Sabbath of the new dispensation, and that the first day *is not*.

———

There is one more text that perhaps could be considered in this connection, though it does not speak of the first day. It is the statement found in Revelation 1:10, "I was in the Spirit on the Lord's day." Some believe that this has reference to Sunday.

It may be confidently stated that nowhere in the Bible, in either the Old or the New Testament, is the first day of the week ever called the Lord's day; nor is it in any way connected with it. There is only one Lord's day, and that is the day which God calls "My holy day," or the Sabbath of the fourth commandment. Isa. 58:13; Ex. 20:8-11.

John was "in the isle . . . called Patmos, for the word of God, and for the testimony of Jesus Christ." Rev. 1:9. As a prisoner he might have been put to work in the copper mines of the island, of which there were many and which were worked by slave and prison labor. Probably, though, because of his age, he was not required to work at all. In any event, on the Lord's day, the blessed day that he so often had enjoyed with the Master, the seventh day of the week, God revealed Himself to John, and gave him those visions that have been the study of God's children ever since.

As stated, there is no Biblical ground whatever for calling Sunday the Lord's day. This contention rests on extra-Biblical grounds which no true Protestant can accept. We rest the case there.

Some Questions Answered

We propose in this chapter to consider some of the questions asked in a previous chapter that deal with the law and the Sabbath. The first of these concerns the abrogation of the law.

Has the Law Been Abrogated?

This question need not take a long time in answering, for we have already partially answered it elsewhere. Is there any statement from the mouth of Christ Himself that answers the question whether the law, or any part of it, has been abolished? This question is important, for it must be clear to all that if the law has been abrogated or changed, then we are entirely out of order in making any argument based on an annulled law. If, on the other hand, the law has not been changed, not even in the smallest particular, then we have all reason to emphasize the ten commandments and consider them binding. We therefore ask Christ: Has the law of ten commandments been abrogated or changed?

The answer comes right back: "Think not that I am come to destroy the law, or the prophets: I am not come to destroy, but to fulfill. For verily I say unto you, Till heaven and earth pass, one jot or one tittle shall in no wise pass from the law, till all be fulfilled. Whosoever therefore shall break one of these least commandments, and shall teach men so, he shall be called the least in the kingdom of heaven; but whosoever shall do and teach them, the same shall be called great in the kingdom of heaven." Matt. 5:17-19.

These are familiar words. They are understandable. Christ here tells us that not one jot or tittle, not the least word or letter, has been changed. Words could not make this plainer.

To this the apostles agree. We quote from Paul, John, and James:

"Do we then make void the law through faith? God forbid: yea, we establish the law." Rom. 3:31.

"He is the propitiation for our sins: and not for ours only, but also for the sins of the whole world. And hereby we do know that we know Him, if we keep His commandments." 1 John 2:2, 3.

"By this we know that we love the children of God, when we love God, and keep His commandments. For this is the love of God, that we keep His commandments: and His commandments are not grievous." 1 John 5:2, 3.

"But whoso looketh into the perfect law of liberty, and continueth therein, he being not a forgetful hearer, but a doer of the work, this man shall be blessed in his deed." James 1:25.

"If ye fulfill the royal law according to the scripture, Thou shalt love thy neighbor as thyself, ye do well: but if ye have respect to persons, ye commit sin, and are convinced of the law as transgressors. For whosoever shall keep the whole law, and yet offend in one point, he is guilty of all. For He that said, Do not commit adultery, said also, Do not kill. Now if thou commit no adultery, yet if thou kill, thou art become a transgressor of the law. So speak ye, and so do, as they that shall be judged by the law of liberty." James 2:8-12.

From this it is clear that the apostles had no idea of any change of the law; they stand just where Christ stood.

The Right to Change the Sabbath

Here is the second question we are to consider: Did God know that a power should arise that would claim the right to change the commandments of God? If so, should not God have forewarned His people; should not God have said something about it in the Bible, so that we might know that He was not taken by surprise, but knew what was coming and provided for it?

To this the answer is that God knows the future, and that hence He knew about the claims which the Papacy would make to change the law of God. A further answer is that God revealed this audacious plan in the Bible long before Christ came to this world.

First, perhaps, we should settle the question of whether the Roman Catholic Church makes the claim that it has power to change the law of God, and in particular, the right to change the Sabbath day. This, of course, is a tremendous claim, even a blasphemous claim. We have noted before that Christ says He is Lord of the Sabbath, indicating clearly thereby that He denies the right of anyone to tamper with the Sabbath. He evidently knew that there would arise men who would claim the power to change the ordinances of God. In saying that He is Lord of the Sabbath, He deprives any man of the right to touch it in any way.

The question has arisen in many minds how men have come to observe the first day of the week as the Sabbath, in plain contradiction to the statement of Scripture that "the seventh day is the Sabbath of the Lord." Our present study will help clear this mystery.

There is probably no more convincing testimony regarding the guilt of a person than the confession of the person involved. In obtaining such a confession, there must of course be no compulsion; it must be a free act, not brought about through or under duress. If a person who has the use of his faculties is accused of a crime, and of his own free will confesses his part in the transgression, there is every reason to accept the testimony as true.

If we apply this principle to the question under discussion, if we ask the accused point-blank if he is guilty or not guilty as charged, if he should answer that he is guilty and should not only willingly furnish the information, but be proud of what he has done and publish his confession far and near, we would be inclined to accept such confession, especially as and if it agreed with known facts. We are therefore going to ask the accused, the Roman Catholic Church, some very definite questions, or rather and better, we are going to let the church ask its own questions and answer them.

The Claims of the Papacy

"*Question.*—Which is the Sabbath day?

"*Answer.*—Saturday is the Sabbath day.

"*Ques.*—Why do we observe Sunday instead of Saturday?

"*Ans.*—We observe Sunday instead of Saturday because the Catholic Church, in the Council of Laodicea (A. D. 336), transferred the solemnity from Saturday to Sunday."—"*The Convert's Catechism of Catholic Doctrine,*" *Rev. Peter Geiermann, C. SS. R., p. 50, 2d edition, 1910.*

"*Question.*—Has the [Catholic] church power to make any alterations in the commandments of God?

"*Answer.*—. . . Instead of the seventh day, and other festivals appointed by the old law, the church has prescribed the Sundays and holy days to be set apart for God's worship; and these we are now obliged to keep in consequence of God's commandment, instead of the ancient Sabbath."—"*Catholic Christian Instructed,*" *Rt. Rev. Dr. Challoner, p. 211.*

"We Catholics, then, have precisely the same authority for keeping Sunday holy, instead of Saturday, as we have for every other article of our creed; namely, the authority of 'the church of the living God, the pillar and ground of the truth' (1 Tim. 3:15); whereas, you who are Protestants have really no authority for it whatever; for there is no authority for it in the Bible, and you will not allow that there can be authority for it anywhere else. Both you and we do, in fact, follow tradition in this matter; but we follow it, believing it to be a part of God's word, and the church to be its divinely appointed guardian and interpreter; you follow it, denouncing it all the time as a fallible and treacherous guide, which often 'makes the commandment of God of none effect.' "—"*Clifton Tracts,*" *Vol. IV, article, "A Question for All Bible Christians,"* *p. 15.*

"*Question.*—Have you any other way of proving that the church has power to institute festivals or precepts?

"*Answer.*—Had she not such power, she could not have done that in which all modern religionists agree with her, —she could not have substituted the observance of Sunday the first day of the week, for the observance of Saturday the seventh day, a change for which there is no Scriptural authority."—"*A Doctrinal Catechism,*" *Rev. Stephen Keenan, p. 174. New York: Edward Dunigan and Brothers, 1851.*

"*Question.*—By whom was it [the Sabbath] changed?

"*Answer.*—By the governors of the church, the apostles, who also kept it; for St. John was in the Spirit on the Lord's day (which was Sunday). Apoc. 1:10.

"*Ques.*—How prove you that the church hath power to command feasts and holy days?

"*Ans.*—By the very act of changing the Sabbath into Sunday, which Protestants allow of; and therefore they fondly contradict themselves, by keeping Sunday strictly, and breaking most other feasts commanded by the same church.

"*Ques.*—How prove you that?

"*Ans.*—Because by keeping Sunday, they acknowledge the church's power to ordain feasts, and to command them under sin; and by not keeping the rest [of the feasts] by her commanded, they again deny, in fact, the same power."—*"An Abridgment of the Christian Doctrine"* (*R. C.*), *Rev. Henry Tuberville, D. D., p. 58. New York: Edward Dunigan and Brothers, approved 1833.*

How will a Protestant answer this challenge?

"You will tell me that Saturday was the Jewish Sabbath, but that the Christian Sabbath has been changed to Sunday! but by whom? Who has authority to change an express commandment of Almighty God? When God has spoken and said, Thou shalt keep holy the seventh day, who shall dare to say, Nay, thou mayest work and do all manner of worldly business on the seventh day; but thou shalt keep holy the first day in its stead? This is a most important question, which I know not how you can answer.

"You are a Protestant, and you profess to go by the Bible and the Bible only; and yet in so important a matter as the observance of one day in seven as a holy day, you go against the plain letter of the Bible, and put another day in the place of that day which the Bible has commanded. The command to keep holy the seventh day is one of the ten commandments; you believe that the other nine are still binding; who gave you authority to tamper with the fourth? If you are consistent with your own principles, if you really follow the Bible and the Bible only, you ought to be able to produce some portion of the New Testament in which this fourth commandment is expressly altered."— *"Library of Christian Doctrine: Why Don't You Keep Holy the Sabbath Day?" pp. 3, 4. London: Burns and Oates (R. C.).*

And here is another challenge:

"The Catholic Church for over one thousand years before the existence of a Protestant, by virtue of her divine mission, changed the day from Saturday to Sunday. We say by virtue of her divine mission, because He who called Himself the 'Lord of the Sabbath,' endowed her with His own power to teach, 'he that heareth you, heareth Me;' commanded all who believe in Him to hear her, under penalty of being placed with the 'heathen and publican;' and promised to be with her to the end of the world. She holds her charter as teacher from Him—a charter as infallible as perpetual. The Protestant world at its birth [in the Reformation of the sixteenth century] found the Christian Sabbath too strongly entrenched to run counter to its existence; it was therefore placed under the necessity of acquiescing in the arrangement, thus implying the church's right to change the day, for over three hundred years. The Christian Sabbath is therefore to this day the acknowledged offspring of the Catholic Church as spouse of the Holy Ghost, without a word of remonstrance from the Protestant world."—*The Catholic Mirror* (*Baltimore*), *Sept. 23, 1893.*

We believe that these statements from recognized Catholic sources are sufficient to prove the point made, that the Roman Catholic Church not only claims to have changed the law of God as regards the Sabbath commandment, but is proud of the fact, and claims that it has done so by divine authority. The church chides Protestants for keeping the first day of the week, for which there is no Scriptural authority, but only the edict of the Catholic Church, when the Protestants claim to accept the Bible and the Bible only.

It appears to us that the Catholic Church is more consistent than the Protestant in this matter. For how can Protestants stand on the Bible and the Bible only and yet accept and obey the voice of the Catholic Church instead of that of Christ? In doing so, Protestants certainly "fondly contradict themselves, by keeping Sunday strictly, and breaking most other feast days commanded by the same church."

Having heard the claims of the Catholic Church that it has a right to change the law of God, and the challenge that is thus made to Protestants to give a reason for their keeping any other day than the seventh day of the week, we would consider the next part of this question; namely, whether God knew beforehand of this apostasy, and what He has to say on the question.

God's Foreknowledge

It is no light thing to attempt to change the constitution of the universe. Such an attempt is the height of rebellion. It strikes at the very heart of the government of heaven. Any treason higher than that could hardly be conceived of. It is undermining the foundations. It is destroying the ground of the atonement, and making of none effect the blood of Christ. A movement such as this, that would eventually gain as many followers as it has, should surely be a subject of prophecy. While it would be presumptuous for man to say what God ought to do, it does seem reasonable to suppose that God would not leave men in darkness to battle alone and ignorantly against such forces and such apostasy.

In this belief we are not mistaken. For God has spoken. We are not left in darkness, nor are we left alone. The whole conspiracy is clearly revealed in Holy Writ. Its inception, progress, and end are faithfully delineated. We need not be misled. All is open to the One with whom we have to do. He has revealed His secrets unto His servants the prophets.

To the prophet Daniel the future was revealed. In

visions of the night he saw the struggles of the saints, the course of world history, the judgment, and the end of all things. He was given a view of a power which was to think itself able to change times and laws, and he saw that this power would have success in its undertakings for a season, until God Himself should intervene. This vision troubled Daniel much. He said, "My countenance changed in me: but I kept the matter in my heart." Dan. 7:28.

As it is not the purpose of these studies to go exhaustively into the prophecies of the book of Daniel, we shall content ourselves with a very brief outline of the chapter under consideration.

Daniel's Prophecy

Daniel, in the vision recorded in the seventh chapter of his book, sees four great beasts, which are explained by the angel to be four kings, or kingdoms, which should arise out of the earth. Dan. 7:17. The fourth beast which Daniel saw was different from the rest, in that it was exceeding dreadful, and had teeth of iron and nails of brass. It also had ten horns, of which three were plucked up. The most remarkable thing, however, was a little horn which came up in place of the three. This horn had eyes like the eyes of man and a mouth that spake great things. This horn "made war with the saints, and prevailed against them." Verse 21. Daniel was especially interested in this horn, for of it the angel said that "he shall speak great words against the Most High, and shall wear out the saints of the Most High, and think to change times and laws." Verse 25. In this he would succeed for a while, but then the judgment would sit and the saints would take the kingdom.

There is general agreement among commentators that these four kingdoms are the four world empires, Babylon, Medo-Persia, Greece, and Rome. "The fourth beast shall be the fourth kingdom upon earth. . . . And the ten horns out of this kingdom are ten kings that shall arise: and another shall rise after them; and he shall be diverse from the first, and he shall subdue three kings." Verses 23-25. Rome, the fourth kingdom, was divided into ten parts, in harmony with God's prediction. It was after this division that another power should arise, diverse from the first, which should subdue three kings. This prophecy found its fulfillment in the Papacy, which was different from the first kingdoms, and which did in actuality subdue three kingdoms in its rise.

We are, in this study, especially interested in the statement that this power should "think to change times and laws: and they shall be given into his hand until a time and times and the dividing of time." Verse 25. The American Translation of the Old Testament published by the University of Chicago reads: "He shall plan to change the sacred seasons and the law." The Septuagint reads: "Shall think to change times and law." Young's says: "It hopeth to change season and law." The American Revised: "He shall think to change the times and the law." Other translations say the same. The word "law" in the Hebrew is in the singular, and doubtless has reference to the law of God, as there would be no point in saying that a certain power should change a human law—a thing that is done continually.

If we are correct in this interpretation, we are face to face with a power that should attempt to change the law of God, written and engraved on stones. This is a most presumptuous undertaking, and could be attempted only by a power that should presume to speak for and act in the stead of Christ. That it must be a religious power is clear from the fact that only such a power would be interested in the law of God.

We have already given the testimony of the Roman

church that it claims the very power to do what the Bible says it shall attempt to do. It is interesting to note that while the church claims to have changed the law and the Sabbath, the Bible does not recognize any such claim, but merely says, "He shall *plan* to change," or, "He shall *think* to change," or, "It *hopeth* to change." The Bible thus affirms Christ's statement that *He* is Lord of the Sabbath. Men may claim the right to change, or that they have changed, the Sabbath. God quietly observes that men may "plan" or "think" or "hope" to change the Sabbath, but they have no power to do so. The wording of this statement in Daniel 7:25 is in itself a weighty testimony to the fact that the Sabbath has not been changed. Men may hope or plan to change it, but God says it cannot be done.

What Protestants Say

It might at this point be interesting to hear what Protestant denominations have to say on this question. Do they recognize the situation as presented by the Roman Catholic Church? Do they know of the claims made, and do they acknowledge them? As long ago as the Protestant Reformation, this was incorporated in the Augsburg Confession:

"They [the Catholics] allege the Sabbath changed into Sunday, the Lord's day, contrary to the decalogue, as it appears; neither is there any example more boasted of than the changing of the Sabbath day. Great, say they, is the power and authority of the church, since it dispensed with one of the ten commandments."—*Augsburg Confession, Art. XXVIII.*

We shall now append quotations from writers who belong to different denominations. They all present the same testimony.

"It is quite clear that, however rigidly or devoutly we

may spend Sunday, we are not keeping the Sabbath. . . .
The Sabbath was founded on a specific, divine command.
We can plead no such command for the obligation to ob-
serve Sunday. . . . There is not a single sentence in the
New Testament to suggest that we incur any penalty by
violating the supposed sanctity of Sunday."—*"The Ten
Commandments," R. W. Dale, M. A. (Congregationalist),
pp. 106, 107. London: Hodder and Stoughton, 1871.*

"There is no word, no hint, in the New Testament about
abstaining from work on Sunday. . . . Into the rest of
Sunday no divine law enters. . . . The observance of Ash
Wednesday or Lent stands on exactly the same footing as
the observance of Sunday."—*"The Ten Commandments,"
Canon Eyton (Church of England), pp. 62, 63, 65. London: Trubner & Co., 1894.*

"And where are we told in Scripture that we are to keep
the first day at all? We are commanded to keep the
seventh; but we are nowhere commanded to keep the first
day. . . . The reason why we keep the first day of the week
holy instead of the seventh is for the same reason that we
observe many other things, not because the Bible, but because the church, has enjoined it."—*"Plain Sermons on
the Catechism," Rev. Isaac Williams, B. D. (Church of
England), Vol. I, pp. 334-336. London: Rivingtons,
1882.*

"It is impossible to extort such a sense from the words of
the commandment; seeing that the reason for which the
commandment itself was originally given, namely, as a
memorial of God's having rested from the creation of the
world, cannot be transferred from the seventh day to the
first; nor can any new motive be substituted in its place,
whether the resurrection of our Lord or any other, without
the sanction of a divine commandment."—*"The Christian
Doctrine," book 2, chap. 7; in "Prose Works of John
Milton," Vol. V, p. 70. London: Henry G. Bohn, 1853.*

"For if we under the gospel are to regulate the time of our public worship by the prescriptions of the decalogue, it will surely be far safer to observe the seventh day, according to the express commandment of God, than on the authority of mere human conjecture to adopt the first."
—*"A Treatise on Christian Doctrine," John Milton; cited in "The Literature of the Sabbath Question," Robert Cox, Vol. II, p. 54. Edinburgh: Maclachlan and Stewart, 1865.*

"I conceive the celebration of this feast [Easter] was instituted by the same authority which changed the Jewish Sabbath into the Lord's day or Sunday, for it will not be found in Scripture where Saturday is discharged to be kept, or turned into the Sunday; wherefore it must be the church's authority that changed the one and instituted the other; therefore my opinion is, that those who will not keep this feast [Easter] may as well return to the observation of Saturday, and refuse the weekly Sunday."—*Extract from the Query to the Parliament Commissioners by King Charles II, April 23, 1647; cited in "Sabbath Laws and Sabbath Duties," Robert Cox, p. 333. Edinburgh: Maclachlan and Stewart, 1853.*

"The Sabbath was appointed at the creation of the world, and sanctified, or set apart for holy purposes, 'for man,' for all men, and therefore for Christians; since there was never any repeal of the original institution. To this we add, that if the moral law be the law of Christians, then is the Sabbath as explicitly enjoined upon them as upon the Jews."—*"A Biblical and Theological Dictionary," Richard Watson, art. "Sabbath," pp. 829, 813. New York: B. Waugh and T. Mason, 1833.*

"The Great Teacher never intimated that the Sabbath was a ceremonial ordinance to cease with the Mosaic ritual. It was instituted when our first parents were in Paradise; and the precept enjoining its remembrance, being a portion of the decalogue, is of perpetual obligation. Hence, instead of regarding it as a merely Jewish institution, Christ declares that it 'was made for man,' or, in other words, that it was designed for the benefit of the whole human family. Instead of anticipating its extinction along with the ceremonial law, He speaks of its existence after the downfall of Jerusalem. [See Matt. 24:20.] When He announces the calamities connected with the ruin of the Holy City, He instructs His followers to pray that the urgency of the catastrophe may not deprive them of the comfort of the ordinances of the sacred rest. 'Pray ye,' said He, 'that your flight be not in the winter, neither on the Sabbath day.' "—*"The Ancient Church," William D. Killen, D. D., pp. 188, 189. New York: Anson D. F. Randolph & Co., 1883.*

These testimonies all agree that there is no Scriptural authority for any change of the Sabbath. They agree also with the Bible on this point; so we accept their testimony as conclusive.

It may now be well to inquire just how the change came about. Some would have us believe that the change came about suddenly. This, however, is not the case. The change was gradual and took some centuries for its accomplishment. Farrar says on this: "The Christian church made no formal, but a gradual and almost unconscious, transference of the one day to the other."—*"The Voice From Sinai," Archdeacon F. W. Farrar, p. 167.* Doctor Killen adds this information: "In the interval between the days of the apostles and the conversion of Constantine, the Christian commonwealth changed its aspect. . . . Rites and ceremonies of which neither Paul nor Peter ever heard, crept silently into use, and then claimed the rank of divine institutions."—*"The Ancient Church," W. D. Killen (Presbyterian), Preface to original edition, pp. xv, xvi. London: James Nesbet & Co., 1883.*

The truth is that for many centuries the observance of

the seventh day continued. On this, Mr. Morer, a learned clergyman of the Church of England, says:

"The primitive Christians had a great veneration for the Sabbath, and spent the day in devotion and sermons. And it is not to be doubted that they derived this practice from the apostles themselves."—*"Dialogues on the Lord's Day,"* p. 189.

Professor Edward Brerewood, of Gresham College, London (Episcopal), says: "The ancient Sabbath did remain and was observed . . . by the Christians of the East Church, above three hundred years after our Saviour's death."—*"A Learned Treatise of the Sabbath,"* p. 77.

Lyman Coleman, a careful and candid historian, says: "Down even to the fifth century the observance of the Jewish Sabbath was continued in the Christian church, but with a rigor and solemnity gradually diminishing until it was wholly discontinued."—*"Ancient Christianity Exemplified,"* chap. 26, sec. 2, p. 527.

The historian Socrates, who wrote about the middle of the fifth century, says: "Almost all the churches throughout the world celebrate the sacred mysteries on the Sabbath of every week, yet the Christians of Alexandria and at Rome, on account of some ancient tradition, refuse to do this."—*"Ecclesiastical History,"* book 5, chap. 22, p. 404.

Sozomen, another historian of the same period, writes: "The people of Constantinople, and of several other cities, assemble together on the Sabbath as well as on the next day; which custom is never observed at Rome, or at Alexandria."—*Id., book 7, chap. 19, p. 355.*

The first legal enactment concerning Sunday took place in the fourth century after Christ, and is known as Constantine's Sunday law.

"The earliest recognition of the observance of Sunday as a legal duty is a constitution of Constantine in 321 A. D., enacting that all courts of justice, inhabitants of towns, and workshops were to be at rest on Sunday (*venerabili die Solis*), with an exception in favor of those engaged in agricultural labor."—*Encyclopedia Britannica, ninth edition, article "Sunday."*

"Constantine the Great made a law for the whole empire (321 A. D.) that Sunday should be kept as a day of rest in all cities and towns; but he allowed the country people to follow their work."—*Encyclopedia Americana, art. "Sabbath."*

"Unquestionably the first law, either ecclesiastical or civil, by which the Sabbatical observance of that day is known to have been ordained, is the edict of Constantine, 321 A. D."—*Chambers's Encyclopedia, art. "Sabbath."*

The law reads as follows:

"On the venerable day of the sun let the magistrates and people residing in cities rest, and let all workshops be closed. In the country, however, persons engaged in agriculture may freely and lawfully continue their pursuits; because it often happens that another day is not so suitable for grain sowing or for vine planting; lest by neglecting the proper moment for such operations, the bounty of heaven should be lost. (Given the seventh day of March, Crispus and Constantine being consuls each of them for the second time.)"—*"Codex Justinianus," lib. 3, tit. 12, 3; translated in "History of the Christian Church," Philip Schaff, D. D. (7 vol. ed.) Vol. III, p. 380. New York: Charles Scribner's Sons, 1893.*

Of this the Reverend George Elliott says:

"To fully understand the provisions of this legislation, the peculiar position of Constantine must be taken into consideration. He was not himself free from all remains of heathen superstition. It seems certain that before his conversion he had been particularly devoted to the worship of Apollo, the sun-god. . . . The problem before him was to legislate for the new faith in such a manner as not to seem entirely inconsistent with his old practices, and not to come in conflict with the prejudices of his pagan subjects. These facts serve to explain the peculiarities of this decree. He names the holy day, not the Lord's day, but the 'day of the sun,' the heathen designation, and thus at once seems to identify it with his former Apollo worship."—*"The Abiding Sabbath," Rev. George Elliott (Prize Essay), p. 229. American Tract Society, 1884.*

However, the church did not want to be left out, and Eusebius, a bishop of the church in the time of Constantine, jubilantly tells of the part the church had in it.

"All things whatsoever that it was duty to do on the Sabbath, these we have transferred to the Lord's day."—*"Commentary on the Psalms," cited in "The Literature of the Sabbath Question," Robert Cox, Vol. I, p. 361. Edenburgh: Maclachlan and Stewart, 1865.*

It was not until later, however, that the church on its own account took legal steps to abolish the Sabbath and institute Sunday in its place.

"The seventh-day Sabbath was ... solemnized by Christ, the apostles, and primitive Christians, till the Laodicean Council did, in a manner, quite abolish the observation of it. ... The Council of Laodicea [364 A. D.] ... first settled the observation of the Lord's day."—*Prynne's "Dissertation on the Lord's Day," pp. 33, 34, 44.*

The text, as quoted by Hefele, is as follows:

"Christians shall not Judaize and be idle on Saturday [Sabbath, original], but shall work on that day. ... If, however, they are found Judaizing, they shall be shut out from Christ."—*"A History of the Church Councils," Vol. II, p. 316.*

Ringgold enumerates these later enactments:

"In 386, under Gratian, Valentinian, and Theodosius, it was decreed that all litigation and business should cease [on Sunday]. ...

"Among the doctrines laid down in a letter of Pope Innocent I, written in the last year of his papacy (416), is that Saturday should be observed as a fast day. . . .

"In 425, under Theodosius the Younger, abstinence from theatricals and the circus [on Sunday] was enjoined. . . .

"In 538, at a council at Orleans, . . . it was ordained that everything previously permitted on Sunday should still be lawful; but that work at the plow, or in the vineyard, and cutting, reaping, threshing, tilling, and hedging should be abstained from, that people might more conveniently attend church. . . .

"About 590 Pope Gregory, in a letter to the Roman people, denounced as the prophets of antichrist those who maintained that work ought not to be done on the seventh day."—*"Law of Sunday," by James T. Ringgold, pp. 265-267.*

In view of all these testimonies, the following statement can hardly be challenged:

"It was the Catholic Church which, by the authority of Jesus Christ, has transferred this rest to the Sunday in remembrance of the resurrection of our Lord. Thus the observance of Sunday by the Protestants is an homage they pay, in spite of themselves, to the authority of the [Catholic] church."—*"Plain Talk About the Protestantism of Today," by Mgr. Segur, p. 213.*

The subject here presented is really a most astonishing one. We are face to face with the fact that the Bible presents one day as the Sabbath, and only one, the seventh day. Catholic and Protestant testimony has been adduced to show that both recognize this fact. Then we have found that the Bible says that a power would arise that should think itself able to change the law. We search for this power and find it, and to our astonishment the power not only admits that it is guilty, but is proud thereof, and points to the Protestant body as endorsing what has been done.

We then turn to the Protestants, and find that they admit that they have no Bible ground on which to stand, but are following custom in this matter. We are perplexed, and wonder how Protestants can stand on the Bible and the Bible only, and yet keep a day not hallowed by God. And no answer to this riddle is forthcoming.

We have already noted that the change from Sabbath to Sunday was not brought about suddenly, but slowly and gradually. It would indeed be true to state that the observance of the seventh day was never wholly obliterated from the church. We can trace the Sabbath through the centuries, and find that here and there companies of Christians observed it even under persecution and trials.

"Down even to the fifth century the observance of the Jewish Sabbath was continued in the Christian church, but with a rigor and solemnity gradually diminishing until it was wholly discontinued."—*"Ancient Christianity Exemplified," Lyman Coleman, chap. 26, sec. 2, p. 527. Philadelphia: Lippincott, Grambo & Co., 1852.*

Grotius adds this bit of information:

"He [Grotius] refers to Eusebius for proof that Constantine, besides issuing his well-known edict that labor should be suspended on Sunday, enacted that the people should not be brought before the law courts on the seventh day of the week, which also, he adds, was long observed by the primitive Christians as a day for religious meetings. And this, says he, 'refutes those who think that the Lord's day was substituted for the Sabbath—a thing nowhere mentioned either by Christ or His apostles.' "— *Hugo Grotius (d. 1645), "Opera Omnia Theologica," London, 1679; cited in "The Literature of the Sabbath Question," Robert Cox, Vol. I, p. 223. Edinburgh: Maclachlan and Stewart, 1865.*

The following two quotations show that the Sabbath was observed by the Celtic Church in Scotland in the eleventh century:

"They worked on Sunday, but kept Saturday in a Sabbatical manner."—*"A History of Scotland," Andrew Lang, Vol. I, p. 96. Edinburgh: William Blackwood and Sons, 1900.*

"They seem to have followed a custom of which we find traces in the early monastic church of Ireland, by which they held Saturday to be the Sabbath, on which they rested from all their labors."—*"Celtic Scotland," William F. Skene, book 2, chap. 8 (Vol. II, p. 349). Edinburgh: David Douglas, 1877.*

The Abyssinians received Christianity in the fourth century through missionaries from the Eastern Church. At that time the Christians had not as yet given up the Sabbath; so the Abyssinians were taught the seventh-day Sabbath and began to observe it. This they continued to do for more than a thousand years, at which time Jesuit priests tried to persuade them to give up the Sabbath and substitute Sunday. A hearing was held at the court at Lisbon, where the Abyssinian legate offered the following explanation:

"Because God, after He had finished the creation of the world, rested thereon; which day, as God would have it called the holy of holies; so the not celebrating thereof with great honor and devotion seems to be plainly contrary to God's will and precept, who will suffer heaven and earth to pass away sooner than His word; and that, especially, since Christ came not to dissolve the law, but to fulfill it. It is not, therefore, in imitation of the Jews, but in obedience to Christ and His holy apostles, that we observe that day. . . . We do observe the Lord's day after the manner of all other Christians in memory of Christ's resurrection."—*Reason for keeping Sabbath, given by the Abyssinian le-*

gate at the court of Lisbon (1534); in "Church History of Ethiopia," Michael Geddes, pp. 87, 88. London: R. Chiswell, 1696.

In Norway Christians kept the Sabbath in pre-Reformation days, as the following shows:

"The clergy from Nidaros, Oslo, Stavanger, Bergen, and Hamar, assembled with us in Bergen at this provincial council, are fully united in deciding in harmony with the laws of the holy church that Saturday keeping must under no circumstances be permitted hereafter further than the church canon commands. Therefore, we counsel all the friends of God throughout all Norway who want to be obedient toward the holy church, to let this evil of Saturday keeping alone; and the rest we forbid under penalty of severe church punishment to keep Saturday holy."—*From minutes of the Catholic Provincial Council, Bergen, 1435 A. D., in "Dipl. Norveg.," 7, 397; cited in "History of the Sabbath," Andrews and Conradi, pp. 673, ed. 1912.*

The work just quoted, "History of the Sabbath," also gives examples of Sabbathkeeping in Sweden, Germany, England, and other European countries in the centuries both before and after the Reformation. With the hundreds of thousands now observing the Sabbath in practically every nation in the world, we believe we are safe in saying that the Sabbath truth has never been entirely obscured, but that every generation has had witnesses for the truth once delivered to the saints.

Under Grace

THE Jews had many feast days and sabbaths which Christians are not to observe. Seven of these feasts are mentioned in Leviticus 23. They include the Jewish Passover, Pentecost, the Day of Atonement, and the Feast of Tabernacles. These feasts were holy days for the Jews, and were called sabbaths, but they are definitely distinguished from the seventh-day Sabbath of the Lord, which is not in any way connected with the ceremonial observances.

"In the seventh month, in the first day of the month, shall ye have a sabbath, a memorial of blowing of trumpets, a holy convocation." Lev. 23:24. The first day of the seventh month might come on any day of the week, the same as the first day of any month does now. Yet it was to be a sabbath. Again, "On the tenth day of this seventh month there shall be a Day of Atonement. . . . It shall be unto you a sabbath of rest." Verses 27, 32. The first day of the seventh month and the tenth day of any month would always come on different days of the week; yet they are both called sabbaths. Throughout the year there were seven feasts coming on different days of the week, and in different months; yet all were sabbaths. But it is distinctly noted, however, that "these are the feasts of the Lord, which ye shall proclaim to be holy convocations, to offer an offering made by fire unto the Lord, a burnt offering, and a meat offering, a sacrifice, and drink offerings,

everything upon his day: *beside the Sabbaths of the Lord."*
Verses 37, 38. A distinction is here made between the
seven yearly feasts and the Sabbaths of the Lord. God
does not confuse them.

It is to these yearly sabbaths that Paul had reference
when he said that they are not to be observed any more.
"Let no man therefore judge you in meat, or in drink, or
in respect of an holy day, or of the new moon, or of the
sabbath days: which are a shadow of things to come; but
the body is of Christ." Col. 2:16, 17.

Compare this text with the one quoted above, and it will
be seen that they speak of the same things, of meats and
drinks and feast days. These feasts are *"beside the Sabbaths of the Lord,"* and are distinguished from them. We
should not confuse the Lord's seventh-day Sabbaths with
the yearly sabbaths of the Jews. They should carefully be
distinguished. The seventh-day Sabbath was included in
the ten commandments written on stone. The feast days
were part of the ceremonial law abolished by Christ.

An Interesting Question

Does not Paul say that Christ blotted out "the handwriting of ordinances that was against us, which was contrary to us, and took it out of the way, nailing it to His
cross"? Yes, Paul says this in Colossians 2:14.

On this text the Reverend Thomas Hamilton, in his
book, "Our Rest Day," which won first prize among the
many essays submitted on the Sunday question in a contest
held in Scotland, speaks as follows:

"To only one other argument on this part of the subject
do we deem it necessary to allude. It is said that Christ,
having by His atoning work satisfied the law of God—that
law is gone, for us, forever. The text is quoted—'Having
blotted out the handwriting of ordinances that was against
us.' Now this argument is simply based on a confusion of

thought. Suffering the penalty of a law does not abolish that law. Nor does perfect obedience to a law abrogate it. But these two things constitute what Christ did. He rendered a perfect obedience to the law, and He bore for His people its utmost penalty. Neither of these two works of His, nor both of them together, amount to anything like the abolition of the law. When a criminal suffers on the scaffold, that means something very different from the abolition of the law against which he has offended. It means the exact contrary. It manifests the strength of the law. His death magnifies the law. No doubt Christ has 'blotted out the handwriting of ordinances that was against us and has taken it out of the way, nailing it to His cross.' The reference in this fine passage is to the practice in Palestine, of a creditor, when his debt was discharged, driving a nail through the bond, to signify that it was canceled. Christ has done that. The ransom has been paid for us, and is not to be paid over again by us. But that act of His only 'magnifies the law, and makes it honorable;' and just in proportion as we appreciate the greatness of the Redeemer's work and enter into its spirit, will we continually honor the law of God in our hearts and lives, not saying that we will have nothing to do with it, but following in His footsteps in this as in all things, and striving to uphold it to the best of our ability."—*Page 63*.

This is excellent testimony, especially in view of the fact that the Reverend Mr. Hamilton's essay was considered by the learned examining committee as being the best of all essays submitted in favor of Sunday, and won first prize.

Another Question

There is another text which we shall now consider. We quote the entire passage, that we may get the setting.

"Him that is weak in the faith receive you, but not to doubtful disputations. For one believeth that he may eat all things: another, who is weak, eateth herbs. Let not him that eateth despise him that eateth not; and let not him which eateth not judge him that eateth: for God hath received him. Who art thou that judgest another man's servant? to his own master he standeth or falleth. Yea, he shall be holden up: for God is able to make him stand. One man esteemeth one day above another: another esteemeth every day alike. Let every man be fully persuaded in his own mind. He that regardeth the day, regardeth it unto the Lord; and he that regardeth not the day, to the Lord he doth not regard it. He that eateth, eateth to the Lord, for he giveth God thanks; and he that eateth not, to the Lord he eateth not, and giveth God thanks." Rom. 14:1-6.

This text, the same as the one quoted above from Colossians 2:16, 17, deals with eating—what may or may not be eaten—and also with days. It has no reference to the seventh-day Sabbath of the Lord; in fact, the Sabbath is not mentioned at all. The argument, as will be seen from reading the whole chapter, deals with judging the brethren, concerning which Paul recommends, "Let us not therefore judge one another any more." Rom. 14:13. It was simply a phase of the old question of "meats and drinks, and divers washings, and carnal ordinances, imposed on them until the time of reformation." Heb. 9:10. It had nothing to do with the Sabbath of the Lord, but concerned such questions as the observance of the day of unleavened bread, the day of the blowing of trumpets, the Day of Atonement, etc. Paul says in effect: "If you wish to observe these days, do so, but do not judge others."

The Two Ministrations

Another passage demands consideration. It is Paul's famous passage in 2 Corinthians 3:1-11.

"Do we begin again to commend ourselves? or need we,

as some others, epistles of commendation to you, or letters of commendation from you? Ye are our epistle written in our hearts, known and read of all men, forasmuch as ye are manifestly declared to be the epistle of Christ ministered by us, written not with ink, but with the Spirit of the living God; not in tables of stone, but in fleshy tables of the heart. And such trust have we through Christ to Godward: not that we are sufficient of ourselves to think anything as of ourselves; but our sufficiency is of God; who also hath made us able ministers of the new testament; not of the letter, but of the Spirit: for the letter killeth, but the Spirit giveth life. But if the ministration of death, written and engraven in stones, was glorious, so that the children of Israel could not steadfastly behold the face of Moses for the glory of his countenance; which glory was to be done away: how shall not the ministration of the Spirit be rather glorious? For if the ministration of condemnation be glory, much more doth the ministration of righteousness exceed in glory. For even that which was made glorious had no glory in this respect, by reason of the glory that excelleth. For if that which is done away was glorious, much more that which remaineth is glorious."

The four expressions which especially concern us are the "ministration of death, written and engraven in stones," in verse 7, which is contrasted with "the ministration of the Spirit" in verse 8; and the other two expressions in verse 9, "the ministration of condemnation," of which it is said that it was "glorious," and the "ministration of the Spirit," which is said to be "rather glorious," and to "exceed in glory."

First, let us agree that that which was written and engraved in stones was the ten-commandment law. Verse 7. Paul says in another place that "the commandment which was ordained unto life, I found to be unto death. For sin, taking occasion by the commandment, deceived me, and by it slew me." Rom. 7:10, 11. The commandments were given unto life. However, if any transgress them, they will be found unto death. Let all take note of this. To the transgressor, the law of life becomes a law of death.

However, it is not the commandments as such that Paul discusses in Corinthians, but their *ministration*. It is the *ministration* of death that is under consideration. What is meant by this?

To teach Israel that it meant death to violate the commandments, the whole sacrificial service was instituted. When a man had sinned, he was to bring his offering, lay his hands upon it, and *kill it*. (See Lev. 4:4, 15, 24, 29.) Note the repetition in these verses, "kill the bullock," "the bullock shall be killed," "kill it," "slay the sin offering." This was all to imprint the seriousness of sin upon Israel. They learned from this that sin meant death.

It is this *ministration* of death which Paul calls "glorious." How could he call it such? Because all the offerings pointed to Christ and to His death, and in that sense were glorious. But more than this. Through these offerings forgiveness was had. When an Israelite brought his offering and confessed his sins, the promise was, "it shall be forgiven them," "it shall be forgiven him," "it shall be forgiven him," "it shall be forgiven him." Lev. 4:20, 26, 31, 35. To be assured of the forgiveness of sin was a glorious experience for the children of Israel. While it was a ministration of death, for the bullock or the lamb was killed, yet the man went away forgiven—a clear and impressive type-lesson of Christ, who should die, and through whose death forgiveness might be had. This is the ministration which Paul calls glorious.

Ministration of the Spirit

But this glorious ministration was to be done away; that is, the whole sacrificial system should be abolished, and another ministration was to take its place. This new ministration is called the ministration of the Spirit and the ministration of righteousness. It is wonderful to be forgiven; but there is something still more glorious. It was wonderful in olden days for a person who had sinned to be able to bring an offering, kill it, and go away with the assurance of sins forgiven. But that, after all, was only typical. The blood of bulls and goats can never take away sin. But the blood of Christ can. We, in this dispensation, need not bring a lamb to be killed. Christ has died for us. He is the Lamb of God. "If we confess our sins, He is faithful and just to forgive us our sins, and to cleanse from all unrighteousness." 1 John 1:9. He is the reality, of which the other was a type. *That* was glorious, for them; *this* exceeds in glory.

But there is more involved than this. The ministration of death functioned only when sin had been committed. The ministration of the Spirit is more glorious, in that it functions to prevent sin. As noted above, it is glorious to be forgiven, but it is still more glorious to be kept from sinning. And this is what the ministration of the Spirit means. "Walk in the Spirit, and ye shall not fulfill the lust of the flesh." Gal. 5:16. This promise is as definite as Paul's other statement, "Sin shall not have dominion over you." Rom. 6:14. Through the agency of the Spirit "the *righteousness of the law* might be fulfilled in us, who walk not after the flesh, but *after the Spirit*." Rom. 8:4. The "ministration of righteousness" is "rather glorious" in that through it the law is *fulfilled* in us rather than *broken* as of old. And so "the Spirit is life *because* of *righteousness*."

We have therefore in Corinthians contrasted two ministrations, one of death—occasioned by the breaking of the law—and one of the Spirit—because of the keeping of the law. The one is a ministry of forgiveness, glorious in itself, but not to be compared to the ministration of the Spirit, which is life because of righteousness, right doing.

These are the two ministrations which Paul contrasts. It is not the *law,* but the *ministrations* of the law, that are the subject. One was of death, because of its transgression; the other was of life, because through the Spirit the righteousness of the law was fulfilled. This passage has nothing to do with the abolition of law, or its change. It discusses only the ministrations.

Nature of Sin

"Sin shall not have dominion over you; for ye are not under the law, but under grace." Rom. 6:14.

There are few more comforting words in the Bible than these, and also few that are more misunderstood. To get the full force of these words in their right setting, let us consider the context.

"Let not sin therefore reign in your mortal body, that ye should obey it in the lusts thereof. Neither yield ye your members as instruments of unrighteousness unto sin: but yield yourselves unto God, as those that are alive from the dead, and your members as instruments of righteousness unto God. For sin shall not have dominion over you: for ye are not under the law, but under grace. What then? shall we sin, because we are not under the law, but under grace? God forbid. Know ye not, that to whom ye yield yourselves servants to obey, his servants ye are to whom ye obey; whether of sin unto death, or of obedience unto righteousness? But God be thanked, that ye were the servants of sin, but ye have obeyed from the heart that form of doctrine which was delivered you. Being then made free from sin, ye became the servants of righteousness." Rom. 6:12-18.

"Sin shall not have dominion over you." Blessed promise! Let every Christian thank God for these words, and may their full significance sink deep into the consciousness of all.

In the whole English language there is no uglier word than "sin." Its mention brings up memories that are painful, saddening, and often heartbreaking. Sin is the cause of all the suffering that is, or has been, or ever will be. There is not a sorrow or a tear, not a heartache or an anguish, but that sin is lurking near as its cause. It is no respecter of persons. It attacks and ruins all alike. No one is exempt from it. If affects not only the one it attacks. Through him it brings sorrow and shame to all his loved ones. It has no redeeming virtue. It is evil and only evil.

God Suffers

One of the strange effects of sin is that the innocent suffer with the guilty. How many mothers there are who have suffered because of their wayward sons! How many wives and children there are who have suffered because of the dereliction of a husband and father! Only eternity will reveal the havoc sin has wrought, and the injustice it has caused.

No one has suffered more than God because of sin, and no one has paid a greater price because of it. A look at the cross of Calvary convinces anyone that the innocent suffer with the guilty, and that none has suffered more than God. But such is the nature of sin. If it were otherwise, it would not be sin.

How could it be imagined that sin could affect the saints in heaven? Or that it could affect God? Yet that is what it has done. Sin caused the Son of God to come down from heaven, to live and die among men. It hanged Him on a cross, pierced His hands and feet with the cruel nails, and broke His heart. The agony of those dreadful hours is symbolic of the agony that has ever been in the heart of God because of sin. On Calvary a fleeting glimpse was given of this supreme sorrow, and then the veil was drawn. But enough was revealed. We know what sin will do; we know what sin has done. If sin had its way, it would again tear Christ from the throne, lacerate His back with stripes, put a crown of thorns on His brow, spit in His face, and then nail Him to the tree. It did this once to God's Son, and it has not changed its nature. Sin is ever the same. What a wonderful thing it will be when sin shall be no more.

It might be supposed that such a monster as sin would always appear repulsive and forbidding. This is not the case, however. Sin is often attractive, even beautiful and alluring. At times it keeps good company, is well dressed, intelligent, vivacious, and highly artistic. Often it is cultured, exhibits good taste, is a lover of music, and delights in the social hour. It hobnobs with bishops and statesmen and the great of the earth, but is, at the same time, at home in the hovel and the brothel. It is generally greeted with pleasure, and is seldom repulsed. It is a universal favorite.

This, however, is true only in the beginning of its acquaintance. It soon changes its attitude. Where it once was ingratiating and agreeable, it becomes repugnant. Where once prevailed beauty, pleasure, and culture, are hideousness, pain, and coarse vulgarity. Gone are its attractiveness and its physical charm. Repulsiveness and coarseness have taken their place.

Go with me to the dance hall: Lithe, swaying bodies in rhythmic motion. Beautiful lighting effect; enchanting music; lively conversation. Athletic young men and charming girls, perfect appointments—little more that heart could wish. Time passes rapidly. It is a wonderful evening. All is like a dream.

Who can imagine that this is the beginning of that which follows? Who can imagine that this is the beginning of sorrow, shame, degradation, suffering? All looks so innocent, so charming. But go with me to another place.

We are in a hospital. There is the girl who, a few years ago, was young, gay, brilliant. Now she is a raving maniac. There is that young man of promise, once so strong, able, ambitious. Now he is wasting away with a loathsome disease. As we look about us we see men and women who once thought that just one drink would do no harm, one fling at unlawful indulgence would have no unpleasant results. They learned too late that the wages of sin is death, often a lingering, horrible death, and that it does not pay to play with fire. They have found, as all will find, that the end of sin is altogether different from its beginning, and that the consequences of transgression are sure and certain. They have learned that the only surety of not having to take the last step is in not taking the first; that the surest cure is prevention.

What can be done about sin? Is there no hope, no help? Must all who are subject to it go down to destruction? Must sin reign forever both in the world and in our mortal bodies? Are we all doomed to hopeless misery and eternal extinction? No, thank the Lord. Sin is no longer to have dominion over us. For we are not under the law, but under grace.

Apart from Christ there is no hope for the human race. Men have battled sin in their own strength for millenniums, but sin has come out victorious. There is no help for sin from any human source. There is help and hope only in God. Thank God that sin shall at last be rooted out, that sin shall not reign in our mortal bodies. Victory over evil, full and complete, shall be ours.

Not Under the Law

"Ye are not under the law, but under grace." The promise that sin shall not have dominion over us is comforting, but the statement that we are not under the law but under grace, is misunderstood by many. By some strange working of the mind, there are those who believe that this statement releases them from fulfilling the moral duties which the law imposes. They believe that the text permits them to observe the part of the law which they approve, and to disregard the part they do not approve. In view of this situation we may rightly ask, What is the meaning of the phrase, "under the law"? Let us illustrate.

A man has committed a serious offense. He flees from the scene of the crime and attempts to hide from the law which he has broken. He is under its condemnation, trembles at the approach of an officer of the law, fearful lest he be recognized, shuns daylight, and feels unsafe even in the dark; in general he leads an unhappy existence. These conditions at last become unbearable, and he surrenders voluntarily; or, as is more often the case, the law catches up with him, and he is placed in prison. He is now not only under the condemnation of the law, but in its custody. His freedom is at an end; he cannot move about any more at will; he is in a cell awaiting the verdict. He is under the law.

This is the first and primary meaning of being under the law. It has two aspects, as may be noted. The first is that of being under the condemnation of the law because of transgression. The second is that of being actually in the custody of the law and deprived of freedom. The experience emphasizes the point that freedom is closely allied to obedience, and that the inscription seen on many courthouses, "Obedience to Law Is Liberty," is more than a catchy phrase. It is a most solemn and important truth.

A man who is thus under the law can be legally freed in one of two ways: He can serve his sentence, at the expiration of which he will again be a free man; or he can receive an official or executive pardon. To be freed on bail, or to be paroled, is only a temporary and conditional freedom and does not come into our present discussion.

If we apply these two ways of gaining freedom to a sinner before God who has broken His law, we immediately recognize that there is no way in which a sinner can serve his sentence and survive, for the wages of sin is death. The only other way, therefore, in which he can ever be freed, is to be pardoned. This pardon God freely extends to those who ask Him in faith, and who fulfill the conditions upon which pardon is granted.

These conditions may briefly be summarized as: (1) sorrow for sin; (2) confession, including restitution where possible and necessary; (3) sincere repentance, including a determination to "go, sin no more;" (4) public acknowledgment of Christ. The fulfillment of these conditions in no way "earns" a man a pardon. They only make it possible for God to extend mercy to him. "If we confess our sins, He is faithful and just to forgive us our sins, and to cleanse us from all unrighteousness." 1 John 1:9. This text records God's promise of forgiveness and cleansing, and also announces the condition upon which it is done.

These considerations bring us to the conclusion that being "under the law" means to be under its condemnation and in its custody, that this condition is brought about by transgression, and that the only way in which a sinner can be freed is by the grace of God. This grace is bestowed freely upon all who will conform to the conditions laid down for full and free pardon.

Pardon and Law

The criminal is under the *condemnation* of the law; the good citizen is not. But both, bad and good, are under the *jurisdiction* of the law. The criminal chafes under such jurisdiction and feels under continual restraint; the good citizen does not feel any constraint. He is hardly aware that there is a law, for he has no urge to transgress it. The one hates the law; the other loves it, for he knows that it is his protector and friend, and that he may appeal to it in case of need. The one looks upon the law as an enemy that threatens to take away his liberty; the other looks upon it as a friend that will protect and guide, and without which neither life nor property is safe.

A man who has transgressed the civil law, been placed in jail, and then graciously pardoned, should not only be deeply thankful to those who pardoned him, but should show his thankfulness by being scrupulously careful of his conduct, so that he never again will come under the condemnation of the law. He should consider that the law that condemned him also pardoned him, and that the law in reality is his friend. This may need elucidation.

A governor has the right to pardon only as the law makes specific provision for it. He may not pardon indiscriminately, but only as the law prescribes. He cannot liberate certain prisoners merely because he is so inclined. He may free them only if the law permits him to do so.

The law, however, does not make pardon compulsory. It does not say that the governor *shall* pardon, but that he *may*. This removes all possibility of a man's ever *earning* his pardon. True, pardon is ordinarily based on good behavior, but good behavior does not *earn* the pardon. All it does is to create conditions that make pardon possible. This distinction is vital, and makes God's pardon, and the ground for it, more understandable.

A Christian is a pardoned sinner. It is the height of folly as well as of ingratitude for such a one to speak "evil of the law" (James 4:11), or hold it in contempt. Such conduct reacts on the Christian, if such he can be called, and raises a doubt in regard to his eligibility to pardon.

Strange to say, there are so-called Christians who do this

very thing. All we can do for such is to pray with Christ, "Father, forgive them; for they know not what they do," and hope that their eyes may be opened to the wonderful goodness of God in pardoning their sins. We can think of no baser ingratitude than that of a man who has been "under the law" and been forgiven, who feels at liberty to violate again the very law for the transgression of which he has just been pardoned. That makes God's grace to him of no effect. It is this very thing Paul feared, when, in the verse immediately following the one that speaks about not being under the law but under grace, he exclaims, "What then? shall we sin, because we are not under the law, but under grace?" This seems so utterly unreasonable to him, that in horror and protest he uses the same emphatic expression that he does in Romans 3:31, "God forbid." Rom. 6:15.

Some were evidently reasoning that if sin gave God an opportunity to manifest His grace, then they had better sin, so that God could have an opportunity to administer His grace. Paul protests this also: "What shall we say then? Shall we continue in sin, that grace may abound? God forbid. How shall we, that are dead to sin, live any longer therein?" Rom. 6:1, 2.

The pardoned criminal is under double obligation to keep the law: first, the ordinary obligation of any citizen to place his influence on the side of law and order; and second, the added obligation because of the mercy extended to him through his pardon. If for no other reason, out of sheer gratitude he is under the most solemn obligation to offend no more.

The pardoned sinner is under like obligation. If, after having been pardoned, he still persists in transgression, he sins not only against the law, but against love, mercy, grace. He was pardoned on the condition, "Go, sin no more." Interpreted, this statement says, "Transgress the law no more," for "sin is the transgression of the law." 1 John 3:4. A man may indeed come short and sin even after his conversion. But he must make sure that his transgression is not willful, done with a "high hand," and he must immediately make his plea for mercy. A pardoned sinner who boasts that he is not under the law, meaning by this that he is not under obligation to keep it, comes near to blaspheming. To him the grace of God has been bestowed in vain.

The true Christian is not under the condemnation of the law, though he is under its jurisdiction. Being pardoned his transgression through the abundant grace of God, he does not go about belittling the law, calling it a yoke of bondage. He loves it. To him it is holy, just, and good. He takes the same position which Christ did toward the law. He does not destroy or break it. He keeps it. "I have kept My Father's commandments, and abide in His love." John 15:10.

God's Sign and Seal

WHEN God delivered Israel out of the Egyptian bondage to make of them a peculiar people, He stated definitely the conditions upon which He would be their God. They were to "do that which is right in His sight, and . . . give ear to His commandments, and keep all His statutes." Ex. 15:26. The commandments here mentioned are the ten commandments, recorded in Exodus 20, and the statutes are the accompanying laws recorded in Exodus 21 to 23.

To test the people, to "prove them, whether they will walk in My law, or no," God proposed to rain manna from heaven for six days each week, but "on the seventh day, which is the Sabbath, in it there shall be none." Ex. 16:4, 26. God commanded them to go out each day to gather the manna, but on the seventh day they were not to go out. By this means He intended to "prove them."

The test was a simple one, as simple as the one given Adam in the Garden of Eden. It was clearly a matter of obedience. But there was no hardship about it. The order could easily be obeyed; and yet it constituted a definite test of man's attitude toward God and His law.

Despite the command given, "there went out some of the people on the seventh day for to gather, and they found none." Verse 27. God now challenged the people: "How long refuse ye to keep My *commandments* and My *laws?*" As far as the record reveals, the people had broken only one command. Yet God accused them of having broken His

13   193

commandments and laws. When they broke the Sabbath, there was evidently more involved than the command in question. It was true then as it is true now, that "whoever shall keep the whole law, and yet offend in one point, he is guilty of all." James 2:10. When Israel broke the Sabbath law, God considered them guilty of disobeying all His commandments and laws.

Because of its peculiar nature, the Sabbath commandment has been God's test throughout the ages. In fact, this seems to have been God's intention from the beginning. He is still proving men, "whether they will walk in My law, or no," by testing them on the Sabbath question. Hear these words of Isaiah: "Blessed is the man that doeth this, and the son of man that layeth hold on it; that keepeth the Sabbath from polluting it, and keepeth his hand from doing any evil." Isa. 56:2.

Here the Sabbath commandment is emphasized, and a blessing is pronounced upon those who keep it. This blessing is extended to "the eunuchs that keep My Sabbaths," and also to "the sons of the stranger, that join themselves to the Lord, to serve Him, and to love the name of the Lord, to be His servants, everyone that keepeth the Sabbath from polluting it, and taketh hold of My covenant; even them will I bring to My holy mountain, and make them joyful in My house of prayer: their burnt offerings and their sacrifices shall be accepted upon Mine altar; for My house shall be called a house of prayer for all people." Isa. 56:4, 6, 7.

The eunuchs were not all Jews, and the strangers were not Jews at all, but foreigners, Gentiles. But to them the promise of the blessing of God was extended on condition of keeping the Sabbath: "Everyone that keepeth the Sabbath from polluting it, and taketh hold of My covenant; even them will I bring to My holy mountain, and make them joyful in My house of prayer."

It cannot be supposed that God would offer these blessings to such as merely kept the Sabbath commandment, but broke the other nine. Rather, God was following His custom of making the Sabbath a test, "that I may prove them, whether they will walk in My law, or no." Ex. 16:4. As Adam and Eve in the garden were told not to eat of the forbidden fruit, and as that was made a test to them of general obedience, so God now makes a test of the keeping of the Sabbath.

Charles Hodge, in his "Systematic Theology," Volume II, page 119, says this of the temptation in the garden:

"The specific command to Adam not to eat of a certain tree, was therefore not the only command he was required to obey. It was given simply to be the outward and visible test to determine whether he was willing to obey God in all things. Created holy, with all his affections pure, there was the more reason that the test of his obedience should be an outward and positive command, something wrong simply because it was forbidden, and not evil in its own nature. It would thus be seen that Adam obeyed for the sake of obeying. His obedience was more directly to God, and not to his own reason."

These are true words. The command to Adam not to eat of the fruit of that certain tree was not the only command he was required to obey. It was simply "the outward and visible test to determine whether he was willing to obey God in all things." So the Sabbath is not the only commandment God wants His people to keep; but it constitutes a test. When men observe the Sabbath, they obey "for the sake of obeying." Their obedience is more directly to God, and not to their own reason.

The Sabbath and Creation

The Sabbath is closely associated with the fact of creation. The majestic words: "In the beginning God created," are a fit introduction to Him who "spake, and it was done," who "commanded, and it stood fast." As a memorial of creation God instituted the Sabbath and asked men to observe it.

In neglecting the memorial of creation, the Sabbath, men are liable to forget both the God of creation and creation itself. Modern higher criticism has almost succeeded in obliterating the God of Genesis, which is the God both of creation and of redemption. The God which the critics worship is not the God of Genesis who in six days made the heavens and the earth, and all that in them is. In so far as their God created anything, He did it millions of years ago, when He made a little spark of life which barely had the power of survival. Through slime, ooze, filth, fight, and chance, this little spark finally became dominant, until it now considers itself able to teach its Maker, contradicting the statements of Him who in the beginning made all things. Critics have no use or room for any "fall" in the Bible sense of the word; consequently there is no need of a Saviour, or Christ. Consistently, there is little need of any "cross," or sacrifice, and men do not need to be "saved." Such, to the critics, are primitive conceptions, which they have long ago outgrown. Evolution is largely non-Christian, if not definitely antichristian.

To prevent, if possible, any such godless theory from gaining foothold, God instituted the Sabbath as a memorial of creation. Had men kept the Sabbath, there never would have been any higher critic, evolutionist, or atheist, for the Sabbath would have been to him a continual reminder of God and creation, and it would each week have provided the needed time for contemplation and worship. This commandment underlies all the others, in that it furnishes the occasion and time for prayer and study, for communion with God and one's own soul, and is thus an incentive to holy living. As Mary, in sitting at the feet of Jesus, chose that good part which should not be taken away from her, so men on the Sabbath have the opportunity as on no other day to sit at the feet of the Master. But this "good part" Satan has attempted to take away, and he has nearly succeeded.

The Sabbath a Sign of Sanctification

The Sabbath is not merely a memorial that points back to creation. It is also a sign of the vital power of present accomplishment—a sign of God's power in the transformation of lives, a sign of holiness, of sanctification.

Says God: "Moreover also I gave them My Sabbaths, to be a sign between Me and them, that they might know that I am the Lord that sanctify them." "Hallow My Sabbaths; and they shall be a sign between Me and you, that ye may know that I am the Lord your God." "Verily My Sabbaths ye shall keep: for it is a sign between Me and you throughout your generations; that ye may know that I am the Lord that doth sanctify you." Eze. 20:12, 20; Ex. 31:13. These texts definitely connect the Sabbath and sanctification. The one is a sign of the other.

Some may wonder what connection there can be between the Sabbath and the Holy Spirit, between sanctification and the keeping of a day. How can the Sabbath be a sign that the Lord "doth sanctify you"? Let us consider this.

Sanctification is the power of God in the individual life so applied that the entire being becomes dedicated to God and His service. It is a Spirit-directed life under the absolute control of God, perfectly yielded and consecrated. It embraces an intense desire for communion with God, a thirsting after the courts of the Lord, a hungering after the divine word that is all-consuming. Christ expressed it in these words: "The zeal of Thine house hath eaten Me up." John 2:17.

Such a life is not an accident, nor is it brought about by the effort or desire of man. It is all of God, who works in us both to will and to do according to His good pleasure. When God has finished His work in us, when He has reproduced His own image in the soul, He puts His seal of approval upon the consecrated life. "He which stablisheth us with you in Christ, and hath anointed us, is God; who hath also *sealed* us, and given the earnest of the Spirit in our hearts." 2 Cor. 1:21, 22. Those who are thus sealed, are "sealed with that Holy Spirit of promise," "sealed unto the day of redemption." Eph. 1:13; 4:30. The Sabbath is the sign of this sanctification. "It is a sign between Me and you throughout your generations; that ye may know that I am the Lord that doth sanctify you." Ex. 31:13. It is God's stamp of approval, impressed upon the heart by the Spirit of God.

For the Sabbath to be a sign of sanctification, it must of course include more than the mere abstinence from labor on a certain day. It is in a very vital sense true, that no unregenerate man can keep the Sabbath holy. He may cease from his common duties, he may even attend divine service, but this does not ensure his entering into the rest of God. Only a Christian can do this. Only "we which have believed do enter into rest." Heb. 4:3. Hence only he who is himself holy can keep the Sabbath holy. True Sabbathkeeping is a spiritual service which can be rendered only by a Spirit-filled person.

God takes cognizance of the thoughts and intents of the heart as well as the outward appearance. As baptism presupposes a spiritual preparation and condition, lest it become merely the washing away of the filth of the flesh, so true Sabbathkeeping presupposes a spiritual preparation and condition, lest the Sabbath become merely a day of indolence and useless inactivity. Let it ever be kept clearly in mind that Sabbath observance is not primarily bodily rest. On the contrary, in many cases it demands greater physical exertion than is required on other days.

To keep the Sabbath day holy means to enter into rest, God's rest. "He that is entered into His rest, he also hath ceased from his own works, as God did from His." Heb. 4:10. God did not rest because He was weary. "The everlasting God, the Lord, the Creator of the ends of the earth, fainteth not, neither is weary." Isa. 40:28. "God did rest the seventh day from all His works," but the rest was first of all a spiritual rest. Heb. 4:4. Even when Adam rested with God that first Sabbath, his rest was not demanded by physical exhaustion. It was primarily a rest with God, a spiritual experience, a day of communion and instruction.

These considerations make it clear that true Sabbath-keeping involves complete dedication to God. The Sabbath is a bit of heaven transferred to this earth. It is a small sample of what heaven will be. The man who keeps it as God would have it kept, must be at peace with God. Not only or merely must his body rest. Rather, his whole soul, body, and spirit must for that day be used in God's service, and everything worldly be shut out.

The mind is probably the last thing of which we will gain complete control. Most Christians can control—some to a greater, some to a lesser, degree—their body and its lusts. Some can control their tongue and their temper, though many fail in this. Few there are, if any, who have reached the standard set by the apostle Paul, who considers the power of God sufficient "to the pulling down of strongholds; casting down imaginations, and every high thing that exalteth itself against the knowledge of God, and bringing into captivity every thought to the obedience of Christ." 2 Cor. 10:4, 5.

199

It is no light thing to bring our thoughts into captivity. Who has not caught himself in church thinking of things utterly unconnected with worship? It is possible for a person to attend divine service on the Sabbath, but his real self, his heart, his mind, his thoughts, be far away. It takes tremendous control, greater than is possible for a human being in any strength he may have of himself, to control his mind. Yet Sabbathkeeping that does not include heart and mind is not Sabbathkeeping in the highest sense.

In perplexity we may all ask, How can this form of Sabbathkeeping be brought about? Is this not an impossible standard? To this it may be answered that we have probably been satisfied with too low a standard of Sabbath observance. Some think that it is sufficient for them to go to church Sabbath morning, and when they have done this, they feel free to do as they please the rest of the day. Others are more conscientious. They would not desecrate the day either by unnecessary traveling and sight-seeing, or by sleeping the precious hours away. Despite this, they find that their minds wander, and that there is little Sabbath in the soul. At times their minds run wild and must be called back again, but even with the best of intentions, they are unable to bring their thoughts into captivity to Christ. Let Sabbathkeeping in its highest sense include a mind *stayed* upon God, a *mind* that keeps Sabbath as well as the body.

To exercise the mind so that it will be stayed upon God is one purpose of the Sabbath. It is a day that should be used in the exercise of godliness, in communion with God, in practicing the presence of God. The man who succeeds in this, who really keeps the Sabbath with all there is of him, has reached the goal God has set for him. He is sanctified, he has reached God's standard. God can put His seal of approval upon him, place His name in his forehead, and exhibit him to the world as a finished product of what Christianity can do for a man. Such a man has used the Sabbath for its intended purpose; it has accomplished for him what God had in mind; it has become the sign and seal of sanctification, and God owns him as His.

"I gave them My Sabbaths, to be a sign between Me and them, *that they might know* that I am the Lord that sanctify them." Eze. 20:12. As men on the Sabbath are instructed in righteousness as they attend worship; as God graciously comes near on that day as on no other; as sins are revealed to them, that they might renounce them; as holiness is held up before them as possible of accomplishment; as the conviction comes to them that Sabbathkeeping must include heart, mind, and soul as well as body; as it suddenly dawns on them that every thought must be brought into captivity to Christ; as the standard is constantly lifted and they cry out unto God for help, men begin to realize the tremendous influence that Sabbathkeeping has upon Christianity. Soon they realize how closely sanctification is bound up with the Sabbath, and how the Sabbath can be a sign *that they might know* that the Lord is their sanctifier. To them Sabbathkeeping and sanctification become synonymous, for they realize that only the man who is completely sanctified can keep the Sabbath as God would have it kept.

While we have stressed the spiritual aspect of the Sabbath, and that it is a sign between God and His people, in another way the Sabbath is a sign to the world. Between God and His people the Sabbath is a sign of sanctification; between God's people and the world the Sabbath is a sign of separation, a mark of distinction between those who obey God, who have come out of the world to enter the heavenly rest, and those who are careless and disobedient. As verily as God in olden times used the Sabbath to "prove them, whether they will walk in My law, or no," so God uses the Sabbath now. Ex. 16:4. This becomes evident from a study of the last church as it is characterized in the book of Revelation.

The Last Church

The fourteenth chapter of this book brings to view a people who stand with the Lamb upon Mount Zion. They are without guile, they are without fault, they are wholly dedicated to God, they follow the Lamb whithersoever He goeth. Verses 1-4. These same people are mentioned in chapter seven as having been sealed with the seal of the living God in their foreheads, and in chapter fourteen they are seen with the Father's name written there. Rev. 7:1-4. Evidently there is a close connection between the Father's name and the seal.

The Holy Spirit is closely connected with the seal of God. "Ye were sealed with that Holy Spirit of promise." "Grieve not the Holy Spirit of God, whereby ye are sealed unto the day of redemption." Eph. 1:13; 4:30.

It should be noted that while these passages do not state that the Holy Spirit Himself is the seal, they do assert that the Spirit is the means which God uses to impress the seal. We are sealed with and by the Spirit of God.

The Greek noun translated "seal" and its verb have in their root meaning the idea of "fencing in," "enclosing," with the purpose of protecting from misappropriation, to keep secure, to preserve. Thus, when a seal is attached to any document, it serves to protect that document from falsification, it fences it in, as it were, attests to its genuinensss, and makes fraud hazardous if not impossible. A seal is also a sign of approval, an attestation of truth and genuineness, a mark of authority and ownership, a proof of quality.

"Him hath God the Father sealed." John 6:27. Christ

is here speaking of Himself. He declares that He has been sealed by the Father. We understand this to mean that Christ had the approval of the Father, that whatever the Son did satisfied the Father and pleased Him, and that He endorsed Christ's work.

In like manner we understand that the 144,000 mentioned in Revelation have the endorsement of the Father. They are sealed with the seal of the living God; they have the Father's name in their foreheads; they are approved of Him. They are without fault; they keep the commandments of God. Rev. 14:12.

The Commandments of God

This latter is important. We believe that we are living in the latter days, and that the church mentioned in Revelation 14 is the last church of God on earth. This is evident from the statements that immediately follow. A white cloud is seen, "and upon the cloud One sat like unto the Son of man," after which follows an account of the end of the world. Rev. 14:14-16. The church that keeps the commandments of God is the last church of God on earth.

The distinguishing characteristic of this church is that it keeps "the commandments of God, and the faith of Jesus." Verse 12. This is a most remarkable statement in view of present conditions. Few churches at this time have much regard for the commandments of God. They are rather inclined to make light of them as well as of those who keep them and teach men so. The chief distinction between those who keep the commandments and those who make light of them, is in regard to the Sabbath. This distinction is as clear now as when God first made the Sabbath a sign, "that ye may know that I am the Lord your God." Eze. 20:20. The Sabbath is still a sign, a mark of distinction, that marks the difference between those who serve and obey the Lord, and those who obey a human enactment sponsored by the man of sin. The Sabbath is a sign "that I am the Lord your God." It is God's sign, His distinguishing mark.

It is interesting to note that the Sabbath commandment is the one commandment in the law which contains the name of the God we serve, and defines Him as the Creator. Other commandments mention God, but the fourth is the only one that distinguishes Him from other so-called gods, and points Him out as the one who in six days made heaven and earth, the sea, and all that in them is.

"The Lord is the true God, He is the living God, and an everlasting King. . . . He hath made the earth by His power, He hath established the world by His wisdom, and hath stretched out the heavens by His discretion." Jer. 10:10-12. On the other hand, "the gods that have not made the heavens and the earth, even they shall perish from the earth." Verse 11. But "I am the Lord that maketh all things, that stretcheth forth the heavens alone; that spreadeth abroad the earth by Myself." Isa. 44:24.

Here God makes a distinction between Himself and other gods, so called. And the distinction He makes is that He is the Creator, He made the heavens and the earth, and He did this "alone." The other gods who did not make the heavens or the earth shall perish.

It is this distinction which the fourth commandment sets forth. And it is the only one of the commandments that does. It points out the true and living God by giving His name, by giving the extent of His kingdom, and by telling us that the God of the Sabbath is the God who created all things, and is therefore the rightful ruler of all. The God "that formed thee" is the same God that "redeemed thee." Isa. 43:1. That is, God is both Creator and Redeemer. "There is no god else beside Me; a just God and a Saviour; there is none beside Me. Look unto Me, and be ye saved, all the ends of the earth: for I am God, and there is none else." Isa. 45:21, 22.

In these texts, as well as in others, creation and redemption are placed together. They are both accomplished by the same God. As a memorial of creation He instituted the Sabbath, and He made this same Sabbath a sign of redemption, "a sign between Me and them, that they might know that I am the Lord that sanctify them." Eze. 20:12. The Sabbath thus becomes a sign of God's total activity, His creative power in the universe, and His re-creative power in the soul. Beside these there are no other powers.

The Sabbath commandment contains all the constituents of a seal: God's name is there; His territory and its extent are mentioned—heaven and earth; His twofold work is recorded: He is Creator, and He is also "thy God"—that is, He is Creator and also Redeemer. These three specifications, the name, the territory, and the work or position of the one whom the inscription concerns, constitute the essential of a seal. They are all found in the Sabbath commandment.

In discussing the seal of God, there is another statement which we should take into consideration. This is found in 2 Timothy 2:19, and reads: "Nevertheless the foundation of God standeth sure, having this seal, The Lord knoweth them that are His. And, Let everyone that nameth the name of Christ depart from iniquity."

The seal, as here described, has two aspects: first, "The Lord knoweth them that are His;" second, "Let everyone that nameth the name of Christ depart from iniquity."

The first inscription informs us that even as the Sabbath is a sign "that *ye may know* that I am the Lord" (Ex. 31:13), so likewise *"the Lord knoweth* them that are His." God's people know that it is not of themselves that they have attained unto sanctification. They know it is *the Lord* who sanctifies them. And *God knows* who they are.

The second inscription informs us that all who name the name of the Lord must depart from iniquity; that is, that all who bear God's name, who have it written in their foreheads, have ceased from sin. They are holy, they are without fault even before the throne of God. Rev. 14:5.

When we now sum up what we have learned concerning the sign and seal of God, we find this: Just before the coming of the Lord in the clouds of heaven, God will have a people, a church, that will reflect His image fully. They will bear His stamp of approval, they will be sealed with the seal of the living God, they will have the Father's name in their foreheads, they will keep the commandments of God and the faith of Jesus. The chief distinguishing mark between them and nominal Christians will be the matter of the Sabbath. This, however, will be more than the matter of a day, for to the church of God the Sabbath is not merely a memorial of creation; it is also a sign of sanctification. They will be a holy people, without spot or blemish, without even a fault. They will know God, and they will be known of Him. They will abstain from iniquity, from sin, and God will approve of them to the extent that He will place His name in their foreheads, and thus they will be sealed unto the day of redemption, sealed with the Holy Spirit of promise, and will bear the sign or seal of sanctification, all of which is included in their keeping the commandments of God and the faith of Jesus. The Sabbath will be the *outward* sign, the mark, the seal, which distinguishes them from those who do not obey or recognize the commandments of God. But to the church the Sabbath will have a deeper significance than that of a distinguishing mark. To them it will mean sanctification, and it will be the sign *between them and God* that marks them as His own.

Sabbath Reformation

"THE seventh day is the Sabbath of the Lord thy God." These words are a part of the fourth commandment as recorded in the twentieth chapter of Exodus. Whatever men may think or do concerning the Sabbath, these words will ever stand as a testimony to the truth of God. The seventh day *is* the Sabbath. In the face of this statement, it is not easy for a Christian to say that the seventh day is *not* the Sabbath. It is too much like contradicting God.

If the question of the Sabbath is as important as our study of it seems to indicate, it might be expected that God in some way will call it to the attention of the world, that all may know and act according to knowledge. It cannot be supposed that God will proclaim the Sabbath to His people as an integral part of the moral law, and then permit this truth to be buried beneath a mass of tradition while an opposing power erects another memorial and palms it off as God's. It is incumbent upon God to see to it that the rubbish is cleared away and the precious jewels of His truth are revealed. We cannot conceive that God reveals truth to the world and then cares nothing about what becomes of it. The same God who gave the seed must see to it that it is watered and bears fruit.

In saying this we are not commanding God or telling Him what ought to be done, but merely reasoning from a human viewpoint. When we then understand that what we are here proposing should be done is exactly what God is going to do, we take courage that it is possible for men to think God's thoughts after Him.

God does not permit His truth to be buried forever. Long before an event takes place—if it is a fit subject for prophecy—God sends word to man concerning it. "He revealeth His secret unto His servants the prophets." Amos 3:7. What is thus revealed may be forgotten, misinterpreted, and rejected, but God, who gave the word, sees to it that in due time proper proclamation is made to the world. When the time draws near, men arise who give the warning, and to the ends of the earth resounds the call of God. God's work is not done, and will not be finished, in a corner. The earth will be lighted with the glory and the knowledge of God, "as the waters cover the sea." Thus it has been, and thus it will be.

The World's Need

The times in which we live indicate the need of attention's being called to the law of God. Lawlessness prevails to an extent unprecedented. It is not sufficient to say that there has always been crime. That, of course, is true. But in the light of modern education and general intelligence, crime has taken on new strength, till it challenges organized government. If to this is added the fact that governments themselves are giving way to forces inimical to the best interests of the state, we see that we are today face to face with a situation that demands a return to law and order, and presages it.

Unless we take the view that God has left the world to shift for itself, we must believe that God gauges His messages to the needs of the hour. There are times when messages of consolation are needed, and God in His graciousness tells the prophet to comfort His people. There are times when reproof is needed, and God speaks sharply to cry aloud and spare not. There are times when disaster is about to overtake a city or a nation, and God sends a message to warn and instruct.

If we were to judge from conditions in the earth today, with lawlessness rampant everywhere, faith disappearing from the hearts of men, and skepticism, cynicism, and agnosticism taking its place, we would say that what the world needs today is the gospel of Jesus, the gospel of faith, hope, and courage for despondent and disheartened humanity, and that the law once more needs to be thundered from Sinai, in all its awful majesty, to impress men that God is in earnest, that the law cannot be flouted with impunity, and that men must return to respect for God's law, or perish. We would say that men need the law preached to them, to awaken in them a sense of sin and condemnation, and also the gospel, in its primitive purity, as a healing balm for bruised souls. The two things, the law and the gospel, are God's appointed means for healing sin's ravages, and, rightly applied, they will cure not only the ills of the individual sinner, but also those of the world.

But, says one, there is nothing new in this. This we admit. There is no other name under heaven given among men whereby we can be saved. There is no new or other remedy than the gospel. As of old, there must be conviction of sin, the individual must be brought face to face with himself in the mirror of the law, he must be made to cry out in agony of soul, "O wretched man that I am!" and then he must receive the precious word of forgiveness and peace.

This simple presentation of the law of God and the faith of Jesus is needed in the world today as much as ever. Men are forgetting the law. It is not preached from the pulpit; it is not practiced in the pew. There was a time when the ministry had an abiding faith in the ten

14   209

commandments as the standard of righteousness. As a result of this belief and its preaching, men had respect, not only for the law of God, but for human law as well. When ministers stopped preaching the law, when they began teaching that it was abolished, men drew the only conclusion that can be drawn from such teaching; namely, that the law is not important, and that it can be broken with impunity.

From this they took another logical step. If the law of God is not important, if the ten commandments are not any longer in force, need the laws of men be respected? We do not believe that in the final reckoning the ministry of today can escape responsibility for the prevailing lawlessness. We have no intention of putting all the blame on them, but we do believe that in a crisis, when the whole world is given over to lawlessness and crime, we have a right to expect the ministry of God to stand for law and order, to lift a mighty voice of protest against sin and transgression, and we do not see how they can consistently do this while repudiating the law of God. We believe that the teaching of the abrogation of the law of God is bearing fruit in general lawlessness, and we would counsel every servant of God who stands in a responsible position to weigh carefully his duty in this respect. If the law of God is spoken of disrespectfully from the pulpit, if the keeping of the ten commandments is considered old-fashioned and incompatible with faith in the gospel, how can anything but disrespect for law be the result of such teaching? How can the teacher escape responsibility? From our viewpoint a grave responsibility rests upon the ministry of today to undo as far as possible the harm that has been done, and to let the voice of God be heard from every pulpit in the land, that God may spare His people and not give His heritage to reproach.

Law and Gospel

But preaching the law—important as that is—is not enough. True, where there has been slackness, there needs to be increased diligence; and where the law has been neglected, there needs to be special emphasis given to it. But nevertheless, the preaching of the law is not enough. The ten commandments need to be thundered, in the ears of sinners, to awaken them to a sense of their condition and to a need of a Saviour; but to preach the law only, and no gospel, will result in despair. The law and the gospel are the two necessary elements in salvation. They are as the two wings of a bird—both needed for flight, one as necessary as the other. They are as the two oars of a boat—both necessary for progress.

The world needs the gospel today more than ever. Where sin abounds, grace needs to abound the more. And sin abounds today. It is not hiding its head and slinking about as in former generations. It is rampant, impudent, aggressive, flaunting its wares, so that all may see. It has entered polite society, it is invited to kings' palaces, it is an honored guest at many banquets, it is an intimate friend in many homes, a popular teacher in many a college. Condemned in the pulpit, it walks arm in arm with the parishioner out of the church; deplored in the legislative hall, it attends the official ball at night by special invitation; outlawed by international agreement, it presides at the armament council; preached against by a thousand bishops, it is pleased to unite with them in repudiating and abolishing the law. Altogether, sin occupies an important place in life today, and in many ways it has succeeded in making itself respectable. This makes its influence all the more insidious, and aggressive warfare against it is imperative.

There is no other help for such conditions than the gospel in its purity and power. Men have tried remedies of all

211

kinds, but have found no help in them. There was a time when it was thought that ignorance was a prime cause of sin, and that education was the remedy. But this has proved a vain hope. Education without the balance of religion may do more harm than good. It may make a good man better, but it tends to make a bad man worse. Where before men were limited in their evil by lack of knowledge, they are now enabled to do much more harm and perpetrate more refined cruelty because of the advantages which modern education affords. An ignorant criminal is a menace; an educated one is a greater menace in proportion to his knowledge.

When we state that the only remedy for the conditions in the world today is the gospel, we do not mean a water-and-milk gospel, an emasculated gospel of sickly sentimentality and spineless platitudes, or an erratic—and sometimes erotic—appeal to unreasoned faith in the supernatural. What we mean is a gospel with some backbone to it, a sturdy faith in a personal God, an implicit trust in a divine Saviour, a humble acknowledgment of personal guilt and an acceptance of pardon, a recognition of duty as well as of privilege, and an aggressive endeavor to help spread the glad news of salvation to the ends of the earth.

As sin takes on new forms, the weapons of the Christian must conform to the pattern of the warfare engaged in. A protective armor is not enough. Weapons for attack are needed also. Christianity is not neutral or negative. It is not phlegmatic or dormant. It is positive, virile, strong, aggressive. As is often the case in real warfare, so in Christian warfare, the best defense is offense. There may have been a time when a kind of negative, yielding goodness was called for. We would not depreciate this. But the time now demands that offensive campaigns be inaugurated, that Satan's stronghold be invaded and his defenses broken down, and that the warfare come out into the open.

Long enough have the forces of Christ taken an apologetic attitude. God now calls for action. We still need the gentle virtues that are always associated with the gospel—perhaps now more than ever. But to this must be added the aggressive "faith that will not shrink," that will do and dare for Christ, the faith of loyalty and optimism, the persistent faith, the victorious faith. The defeatist attitude must be conquered, the apologetic mien discarded, and God's church must go forward in the strength of a sure purpose, bearing aloft the banner: THE COMMANDMENTS OF GOD AND THE FAITH OF JESUS.

The Commandments of God

This last expression is taken from the book of Revelation, and describes exactly what is needed today. The whole text reads: "Here is the patience of the saints: here are they that keep the commandments of God, and the faith of Jesus." Rev. 14:12. In this the complete gospel is revealed, the gospel for such a time as this. Let us examine the statement.

"Here is the patience of the saints." The word "saints" is the same word that is in other places translated "holy," the Greek *hagios*. It is used in such expressions as "holy Father," "holy child Jesus," "temple of God is holy," "holy and without blemish," "present you holy and unblamable," "He which hath called you is holy," "holy men of God spake," "holy is His name." John 17:11; Acts 4:27; 1 Cor. 3:17; Eph. 5:27; Col. 1:22; 1 Peter 1:15; 2 Peter 1:21; Luke 1:49. We are therefore safe in believing that the ones here spoken of are saints in the truest sense, that they are sanctified and holy, without spot, and blameless.

The saints that are thus spoken of keep the commandments of God and the faith of Jesus. To some this may seem like a strange statement, because popular theology does not combine the keeping of the commandments with holiness. Rather, many who claim holiness repudiate utterly the commandments of God, and seem to hold themselves aloof from anything that savors of law. But not so God. When He wishes to define those who are truly holy, when He wishes to point out those who are really holy in the sight of heaven, He says that they keep the commandments of God. True sanctification and the commandments belong together.

The chapter from which we quote the text under consideration begins by giving a description of the Lamb of God standing on Mount Zion, "and with Him a hundred forty and four thousand, having His Father's name written in their foreheads." Rev. 14:1. They are spoken of as "they which were not defiled with women; for they are virgins. These are they which follow the Lamb whithersoever He goeth. These were redeemed from among men, being the first fruits unto God and to the Lamb. And in their mouth was found no guile: for they are without fault before the throne of God." Verses 4, 5. They are the same as those "that keep the commandments of God, and the faith of Jesus." Verse 12. They are doubtless also the same as those that are mentioned in Revelation 12:17 as "the remnant of her seed, which keep the commandments of God, and have the testimony of Jesus."

This remnant is generally considered to be the last of God's people on earth, those who live just before the appearing of the Son of God in the clouds of heaven. The word "remnant" would seem to indicate this, though we are not dependent upon that expression alone for this view. The whole context gives the same impression. The messages of the three angels mentioned in Revelation 14 are the last messages sent to the earth before the coming of the Lord. Immediately following their proclamation, John says: "I looked, and behold a white cloud, and upon the cloud one sat like unto the Son of man, having on His head a golden crown, and in His hand a sharp sickle. . . . And He that sat on the cloud thrust in His sickle on the earth; and the earth was reaped." Verses 14-16. It therefore seems clear that the remnant of God's people, those who live just before the coming of the Son of man, the last generation on earth, will have attained unto holiness of life, and they will keep God's commandments.

We believe that we are living near the time when we may expect to see the Son of man come in the clouds of heaven. It is at such a time that the distinguishing mark of those who are sanctified is that they keep the commandments. It is therefore evident that the law must have come into its own again. Before a people can be produced who keep the commandments, there must be a preaching of the commandments, there must be an awakening on the part of the people to the binding claims of God's law. We may therefore rightly look for a revival of the study of the law before the coming of the Lord, and this revival will be so widespread as to take in all nations and peoples, out of which the remnant will be taken.

We might expect more than this. As the people study the law, they will naturally have their attention called to the fact that they are not keeping holy the day which the commandment demands. This will lead them to a thorough search for truth, and this search will lead them to other truths which have been hidden for ages and generations. As the truth of the seventh-day Sabbath dawns upon them, they will naturally be led to consider the question of creation, which is closely bound up with it. Being believers in the Bible, they will take their stand upon the account given in Genesis in regard to creation, and will be diametrically opposed to any doctrine that is evolutionary in origin or in tendency.

Thus a people will be developed who are Bible Christians, Fundamentalists, who keep the commandments of God and observe the seventh day as the Sabbath. These people will be sealed with the seal of God; they will have the Father's name in their foreheads, and will be without spot or wrinkle or any such thing. They will be faultless before the throne of God.

The Patience of the Saints

Read again the description of the people who meet with God's approval: "Here is the patience of the saints: here are they that keep the commandments of God, and the faith of Jesus." Note: they are saints, that is, they are sanctified, they are holy. They have patience, or, as the word denotes, endurance, strength, tenacity. They keep the commandments. They have faith.

The first characteristic here mentioned is that of patience. This word has been misunderstood in that it is generally thought to mean the opposite of impatience. It is not denied that it has this meaning, but only in a secondary or minor sense. The word ordinarily has a larger significance, which perhaps is best translated "endurance." Young translates it thus, and also Rotherham. The American Revised Version has in the margin "steadfastness." In the text: "Let us run with patience the race that is set before us" (Heb. 12:1), the meaning is not that we must not be impatient in running, but that we must run with endurance, with courage, with steadfastness, that we must not give up, but keep on, whatever the obstacles may be.

The word has the same meaning in Hebrews 10:36: "Ye have need of patience, that, after ye have done the will of God, ye might receive the promise." The meaning here is not that we must not become impatient—though that is true—but rather that if we are to receive the promise, we must have endurance, we must not give up, we must steadfastly continue. In all but two cases in the New Testament the word has the same meaning.

When our text, therefore, speaks of the patience of the saints, it refers to their steadfastness, their perseverance, their "undiscourageableness," their optimism, their endurance. Thus the word is a whole history in itself of what the saints have passed through. They have been tried to the utmost. They have been tempted to give up. They have stood face to face with obstacles which seemed insurmountable. But they would not be discouraged. They would not give up or give in. When hope faded, and it seemed that they could not hold out any longer, they did not falter. With Christ, they decided that they would neither fail nor be discouraged.

The verses that precede Revelation 14:12 give some clue to the struggle through which the saints have passed. They have been faced with the alternative of receiving the mark of the beast in their forehead or in their hand, or being killed. Rev. 14:9; 12:15-17. They have had to face the question of worshiping the beast and receiving his mark, of being unable to buy or sell. Rev. 12:17. If they did *not* worship the beast, the decree of the beast was that they should be killed. If they *did* worship the beast, God decreed that they should drink of the wrath of God. Rev. 14:15, 10. This placed them in a serious dilemma. But they did not falter. When the struggle was over, they had in their forehead, not the mark of the beast, but the Father's name. Rev. 14:1. They had gained complete victory. They had not given up. They had persevered. They had shown that they could stand any test placed upon them. They had the patience, the steadfastness, the endurance, of the saints.

We have already discussed the second statement in our texts, that these people are saints, sanctified, holy. They have been in Babylon, but have come out of it. Rev. 14:8;

18:4, 5. In times when men and nations drank "of the wine of the wrath of her fornication," they "were not defiled with women; for they are virgins." Rev. 14:8, 4. Under great stress and temptation they remained pure, physically and spiritually. They were saints, but not because they had been shielded from temptations, for they had been exposed to every form of it, and had been threatened unless they yielded. But nothing could move them. They knew in whom they believed, and they remained firm.

These saints keep the commandments. There must be something of special significance in this statement. In view of the times in which they live, there can be only one commandment to which reference could be intended. No Christian would think of stealing or swearing and not be ashamed of it. It is unthinkable that a Christian would consider it praiseworthy to break the seventh commandment. But when it comes to the seventh day, the case is different. That day some break and yet consider themselves good Christians. How can this be? Why break one commandment and not the others? The saints "keep the commandments." One of these commandments is the fourth. They keep that with the rest. They keep all.

The Sabbath Restored

An interesting text is found in the fifty-eighth chapter of Isaiah, to which we would at this time call attention. The whole chapter is addressed to God's people who are showing a commendable interest in many things, but who come short in some vital matters.

The prophet is told to show God's people "their transgression, and the house of Jacob their sins." They seek the Lord daily, and delight to know His ways and to approach God. Verses 1, 2. But they are perplexed that God does not seem to recognize them. "Wherefore have we fasted, say they, and Thou seest not? wherefore have we afflicted our soul, and Thou takest no knowledge?" Verse 3. They are what could be called good people; they delight in God and in His service; they afflict their souls. But there is something wrong, for God does not see or take knowledge of them.

The Lord now calls attention to their shortcomings. If they really want to know why God keeps aloof, He will let them know. They have enjoyed themselves while others have suffered. They have fasted, indeed, but it has not been the kind of fast that is pleasing to God. The real fast, God says, consists in doing good, in helping the poor, in relieving the oppressed, in sharing our bread with the hungry, and in clothing the naked. If the people will do this, great blessing will come to them. Their health shall return, light from God shall come to them, righteousness and glory shall be their rearward, and God will again hear their prayers and draw near to them. Their souls shall be satisfied in drouth, and the Lord shall guide them continually. Verses 6-11.

Now comes the text to which we would call special attention. "They that shall be of thee shall build the old waste places: thou shalt raise up the foundations of many generations; and thou shalt be called, The repairer of the breach, The restorer of paths to dwell in. If thou turn away thy foot from the Sabbath, from doing thy pleasure on My holy day; and call the Sabbath a delight, the holy of the Lord, honorable; and shalt honor Him, not doing thine own ways, nor finding thine own pleasure, nor speaking thine own words; then shalt thou delight thyself in the Lord; and I will cause thee to ride upon the high places of the earth, and feed thee with the heritage of Jacob thy father: for the mouth of the Lord hath spoken it." Verses 12-14.

This brings us to the Sabbath question again. The people mentioned in this chapter have not made a practical application of their Christianity. They have not been as interested in the poor and unfortunate as they should be. The counsel given them is that they are to take a personal interest in the poor and needy. They are not only to give a dime or a dollar to the hungry; they are to divide their own loaf with them. They are not to send the homeless to some institution. They are to take them to their own house. They are to take personal interest in those for whom they work. They are to make their Christianity practical, and take a part in the work themselves, and not do it all by proxy.

Also, they are not to forget the Sabbath. This counsel comes as a parting admonition, so that they will remember it. Doing so they will "raise up the foundations of many generations." They will be called, "The repairer of the breach, The restorer of paths to dwell in." This is to be "if thou turn away thy foot from the Sabbath"—that is, cease to trample the Sabbath underfoot, "from doing thy pleasure on My holy day; and call the Sabbath a delight, the holy of the Lord, honorable."

Note what God here calls the Sabbath. It is called "My holy day," "a delight." It is called "the holy of the Lord, honorable." The word "holy" here used is the Hebrew *qadosh,* the same word which the angels use when they say: "Holy, holy, holy, is the Lord of hosts." Isa. 6:3. The word "honorable," Hebrew, *kabed,* means to make heavy or weighty, to place stress upon, and thus to honor. No other interpretation can be placed upon these expressions than that God highly honors the Sabbath day and wants His people to honor it.

"And shalt honor Him," rather, "it." This is the way the American Revised, Young's, American Translation, Variorum, and others have it. "And shalt honor it," the Sabbath. Both translations may be correct, for whoever honors the Sabbath also honors the Lord of the Sabbath.

All who thus honor the Sabbath shall delight themselves in the Lord and ride upon the high places of the earth. "The mouth of the Lord hath spoken it."

We now ask in all seriousness: Is it reasonable to suppose that God would thus speak of the Sabbath, lauding it in the highest terms, calling it "My holy day," warning us not to trample it underfoot, and then not mean it? Can we believe that He would call it "honorable," put weight upon it, ask us to delight in it; can we believe that He would give it the distinctive title, "the holy of the Lord," and promise great blessings to those who will honor it, and then throw it into discard? We do not see how this can be.

The Breach

But note again. Those who thus honor the Lord in restoring the Sabbath to its proper place will be called "The repairer of the breach, The restorer of paths to dwell in." Isa. 58:12. This calls for some consideration.

"The repairer of the breach." In ancient times the cities were surrounded by walls. In besieging a town the enemy would seek to make a breach in the walls through which an attack could be made. Battering rams would be placed so that they would tear down part of the wall and make a gap through which the soldiers could enter and take the town. Whenever such a breach was made, the battle would rage around that particular spot. The rest of the wall would be practically deserted, and both sides would concentrate on the breach. Those who tried to repair the breach would expose themselves to danger, but should they be successful, great would be their reward.

This is the picture presented to us in the phrase, "repairer of the breach." The statement is closely associated with the Sabbath and with the law of God; so it might be well to connect it with what the prophet Ezekiel has to say on the same subject.

"Her priests have violated My law, and have profaned Mine holy things: they have put no difference between the holy and profane, neither have they showed difference between the unclean and the clean, and have hid their eyes from My Sabbaths, and I am profaned among them." Eze. 22:26. This is a serious charge against the priests of God. They have not been faithful. They have violated the law. They have hid their eyes from the Sabbath, and God is profaned among them.

They have done more. They have "daubed them with untempered mortar, seeing vanity, and divining lies unto them, saying, Thus saith the Lord God, when the Lord hath not spoken." Verse 28. It is a very serious charge against the ministry which God makes. He charges them with saying, "Thus saith the Lord God, when the Lord hath not spoken." This charge must have something to do with the Sabbath, for that is one of the matters under consideration.

"I sought for a man among them, that should make up the hedge, and stand in the gap before Me for the land, that I should not destroy it: but I found none." Verse 30. God says that He looked for a man among them to "stand in the gap." But He found none. The word "gap" is the same word, *perets* in Hebrew, that is translated "breach" in Isaiah. In Isaiah God calls those who are faithful, "repairer of the breach." In Ezekiel He looks for a man among the priests who will stand in the breach. But He finds none. Both statements are made in connection with the Sabbath question. The connection and the illustration are very apt.

The law of God is a protection to His people. It is as a wall about the saints. It is the dividing line between the world and the church. Inside is the church; outside is the world. As long as the keeping of the commandments is a requisite for entrance into the church, all is well. But if a breach should be made in the wall, the enemy would find easy access, and would stream into the church. This is in reality what has happened. The law has been broken down, a breach has been made, and now there is very little difference between those who are outside and those who are inside.

God is looking for men who will stand in the gap and make up the hedge. As He looks among the priests, He finds that they are violating the law and are hiding their eyes from the Sabbath. Instead of helping repair the breach, they are attempting to build another wall of their own. Of them God says: "They have seduced My people, saying, Peace; and there was no peace; and one built up a wall, and, lo, others daubed it with untempered mortar." Eze. 13:10.

We have proceeded far enough to make the necessary application. The wall is the law of God, the ten commandments. This wall men have broken down, and the breach has been made in it. The place where the attack has been made and the breach attempted, is the fourth commandment, the seventh-day Sabbath. For ages and generations this breach has existed, and God has sought for men to repair it, but He has found none. Because of the breach in the law, men have surged into the church, unconverted men, till there is now practically no difference between the church and the world.

But this condition will not continue forever. God will find some at last who will stand in the breach and make up the hedge. They will be called "The repairer of the breach, The restorer of paths to dwell in." They will "keep the commandments of God, and the faith of Jesus." They will call the Sabbath "a delight, the holy of the Lord, honorable." And the gap will be made up, the breach will be stopped. God's people will again be inside the protecting walls of His holy law, and the transgressors outside. There is only one way to get in. That is through the door, Christ Jesus. None but converted people can get in. Only those called to be saints are admitted. The others must stay outside.

What do these others do? They build another wall, a "slight wall," as the correct marginal reading is in Ezekiel 13:10. This wall they daub with untempered mortar, to make it look better. Untempered mortar is mortar that has not been properly prepared, and that hence will not stand the tests when the storm comes. So these priests who violate the law and hide their eyes from the Sabbath build up another wall—really a partition only—but they daub it with untempered mortar, so that the unwary will be deceived and will think that it is substantial. It does not need much imagination to understand what this wall is. It is the spurious law which men try to substitute for God's law, commanding men to keep, not the Sabbath of the Lord, the seventh day, but Sunday, the counterfeit sabbath of men's devising. The untempered mortar is the fallacious argument for Sunday sacredness that will not stand the test to which it will be put.

What will happen to this wall that is thus built up? Let God speak: "Say unto them which daub it with untempered mortar, that it shall fall: there shall be an overflowing shower; and ye, O great hailstones, shall fall; and a stormy wind shall rend it. Lo, when the wall is fallen, shall it not be said unto you, Where is the daubing wherewith ye have daubed it? Therefore thus saith the Lord God: I will even rend it with a stormy wind in My fury; and there shall be an overflowing shower in Mine anger, and great hailstones in My fury to consume it. So will I break down the wall that ye have daubed with untempered mortar, and bring it down to the ground, so that the foundation thereof shall be discovered, and it shall fall, and ye shall be consumed in the midst thereof: and ye shall know that I am the Lord. Thus will I accomplish My wrath upon the wall, and upon them that have daubed it with untempered mortar, and will say unto you, The wall is no more, neither they that daubed it; to wit, the prophets of Israel which prophesy concerning Jerusalem, and which see visions of peace for her, and there is no peace, saith the Lord God." Eze. 13:11-16.

This is what God will do with the wall that men build: I "will break down the wall;" "I will . . . rend it with a stormy wind in My fury; . . . it shall fall, and ye shall be consumed in the midst thereof;" I will "accomplish My wrath upon the wall, and upon them that have daubed it with untempered mortar." At last "the wall is no more, neither they that daubed it."

These verses portray God's feeling toward those who try to make a substitution for God's law. God is jealous for His Sabbath. He wants men to honor it. He tries to get men to make up the hedge and stand in the gap, but among the priests He finds none. Instead of helping to repair the breach, they attempt to build another wall. This arouses God's wrath. The storm comes, and the wall goes down. It looked beautiful; it was daubed all over with untempered mortar; but it could not stand the storm. The end was complete destruction.

Two Groups

How true to fact is this prophetic picture of what is going on in the world today! Men have rejected the Sabbath of the Lord and have substituted a spurious sabbath. This they daub with all kinds of specious arguments to make it look substantial and good, but to no avail. At last it will go down, and they that daub it will go down with it.

On the other side are the people of God. They are restoring the old paths, they are repairing the breach, they are standing in the gap. They delight in the Sabbath, they keep the commandments, they endure unto the end. They are the true saints of God.

Men are now deciding which group to join. On the one hand is a small group who are repairing the breach in the rugged old wall and restoring the inscription on it. On the other hand is a much larger group who are trusting to a flimsy partition that sways in the wind, hoping that it will protect them from the storm that is coming. From the vantage point of God's word we know the outcome. The little group shall "ride upon the high places of the earth;" the larger group will go down to destruction when the overflowing scourge shall come. Isa. 58:14; Eze. 13:13, 14.

Our consideration thus far has led us to the belief that there will be a very definite and widespread Sabbath reformation before the Lord appears in the clouds of heaven. This is as it should be, and is in harmony with God's general plan of working. Very seldom does God interfere immediately with the plans of men. They are given time to develop their ideas, that the results may become apparent. We believe, however, that the time has now come for God to interfere. "It is time for Thee, Lord, to work; for they have made void Thy law." Ps. 119:126.

As we look about us in the world today, we find definite indications that God is doing the work foretold by prophecy. All over the earth men and women are calling attention to the commandments of God and the faith of Jesus. In spite of opposition and hardships, thousands and tens of thousands are every year joining the ranks of those who in all humility follow the footsteps of the Master. They have no special wisdom or influence, but through them God has done and is doing a work that is a marvel among men. In every land they are found. Their mission stations are found in the frozen north and on the burning sands. Drouth, depression, and hardship are not obstacles. Their work goes on. A hundred thousand youth are found in their schools, getting ready to step into the places made vacant by older workers, and to carry on the work to even greater victory. Nothing can stop this movement. It has the stamp of God's approval. It will triumph.

The Faith of Jesus

The saints mentioned in Revelation 14:12 not only keep the commandments of God, but also have the faith of Jesus. A few words concerning this might not be amiss at this juncture.

The statement that the saints keep the faith of Jesus might perhaps better read "faith in Jesus," as the Greek denotes, or it might even mean the faith taught by Jesus. For our present purpose we might keep the reading "faith of Jesus," having in mind that it includes both faith in Jesus and also the faith taught by Him.

The fact that the statement says that the saints keep the commandments of God and also the faith of Jesus shows that it does not refer to the old dispensation. The saints are New Testament Christians. They keep the faith of Jesus; they follow the Lamb whithersoever He goeth.

In a time of doubt and unbelief it is well to keep the faith. Some people have lost faith in almost everything. And not without reason. They had faith in banks. These failed. Some had faith in governments. These failed. Some had faith in the church. It has failed. Some had faith in their own power to pull them through. That failed. On every hand there is failure. Men have lost faith in mankind, in the orderly processes of nature, in themselves, in God. "When the Son of man cometh, shall He find faith on the earth?" Luke 18:8. To this the answer is that He will find faith. There are some who keep their faith in Jesus.

Do not all Christians have faith in Jesus? No, they do not, if by Christians are meant such as are members of the church. What does it mean to have faith in Jesus? It means the same as when we say that we have faith in certain people; that is, we trust them and believe in their word. We rely on their promise; we accept their statements as true. Do not all so-called Christians have such faith in Christ? No, they do not. Hear the complaint of Jesus: "Why call ye Me, Lord, Lord, and do not the things which I say?" Luke 6:46. It is of no use to claim great faith in God, and not do the things which He commands. Faith and obedience are closely related, so closely that they cannot be separated.

Christ's statement, as quoted by Luke, strikes at the very root of an important principle in the Christian religion. Christ says, in effect: Of what use is it to take My name, to call yourself a Christian, if you do not do what I say? There are many today who say, Lord, Lord, but do not do. Christ raises the question of the value of a profession without corresponding works.

We do not suppose that this "doing" has reference to any one thing. Rather, it has reference to all our Christian duties. It strikes particularly at such as deny that there is any virtue in doing anything; who hold up their hands in horror when it is suggested that the commandments of God are a guide to life's duties, and should be kept. This attitude is common among some apparently devoted, but misguided, people. The last chapter of the last book of the Bible contains this parting admonition: "Blessed are they that do His commandments, that they may have right to the tree of life, and may enter in through the gates into the city." Rev. 22:14.

Faith is not inconsistent with works. Rather, doing is a

part of faith, for it is by doing that we show our faith. It is to this that Christ refers when He questions the faith of those who call Him, "Lord, Lord," but will not do. "Faith without works is dead," says James.

The saints have "the faith of Jesus;" that is, the kind of faith He had, the kind He taught. There could not be a better faith than that. If we were asked to give a sure and certain rule of faith and practice, we could not give a better answer than this: "Follow the footsteps of the Master; accept and hold the kind of faith He had."

If we look once more at the four things mentioned in Revelation 14:12, we see clearly what God expects of His people in these last days, and also the possibility of attaining that which God demands. The text reads: "Here is the patience of the saints: here are they that keep the commandments of God, and the faith of Jesus." The four things which characterize God's true people are: first, they have patience, they endure, they are steadfast; second, they are holy, sanctified, consecrated saints; third, they keep the commandments, which means that they keep all ten, including the fourth, the Sabbath commandment; fourth, they have the faith of Jesus; that is, they believe in Him, they follow Him, they not only *say,* "Lord, Lord," but they *do* what He says.

This describes the saints of God who will constitute the last people on earth, the remnant, those who live just before the coming of the Son of man in the clouds of heaven. The wording of the text answers the question in the minds of some in regard to whether it is really possible to keep the law of God.

Some confidently assert that it cannot be done. One can almost hear the challenging objections: It is impossible to keep the law of God. Show me a man who has ever done it or who can do it. You claim that it can be done. Where are they who do it? The answer comes ringing back: Here they are. "Here are they that keep the commandments of God, and the faith of Jesus."

God knows those who are His. They have the Father's name in their foreheads; they are sealed with the seal of God. They follow the Lamb; they keep the commandments. It would be well for all to check their lives against the requirements of God, and make sure that they measure up to the demands of God for this time.

The Final Controversy

THERE has always been warfare between good and evil. In the very nature of the case this must be so. The first promise in the Bible contains these words of God: "I will put enmity between thee and the woman." Gen. 3:15. This enmity is God ordained. As long as sin exists, this enmity will endure. It cannot be otherwise.

We do not know when the original controversy between good and evil began in heaven, but it must have been before Adam and Eve were created. In any event, after Satan had sinned, "there was war in heaven: Michael and His angels fought against the dragon; and the dragon fought and his angels." Rev. 12:7. This warfare, after being transferred to the earth, has continued until the present time, and will culminate in the last great conflict, when Satan will "make war with the remnant of her seed, which keep the commandments of God, and have the testimony of Jesus." Verse 17.

Lucifer

As for the cause of the beginning of the conflict, we have a few hints in the Bible. Satan, or Lucifer, as he was then called, had a very high position in the heavenly courts, perhaps the highest of all created beings. He was one of the two anointed cherubs that covered. The statement reads: "Thou art the anointed cherub that covereth." Eze. 28:14. In the most holy place in the sanctuary on earth

231

there were two angels made of gold that stood with out-spread wings covering the mercy seat, beneath which was the law of ten commandments. Ex. 25:20; 37:9; 1 Chron. 28:18. These two angels represent the angelic host who surround the throne of God, and who stand in His immediate presence. The word "covereth" here means to hedge in, to protect. The Douay Version translates: "Thou, a cherub stretched out and protecting." Eze. 28:14. Lucifer was one of these cherubs in the real sanctuary above. His work was to hover over, to protect, the oracles of God.

We would call attention to another statement which throws some light on the career of Lucifer. This is the statement: "Thou sealest up the sum, full of wisdom, and perfect in beauty." Eze. 28:12. "Thou sealest up the sum." The reading here is admittedly difficult. It may mean, as some think, that Lucifer in himself sealed up all that is perfect, that he was complete, without fault. If so, the statement would be in harmony with that which immediately follows: "Full of wisdom, and perfect in beauty."

There is another rendering which to us seems more nearly correct. The Hebrew word *toknith,* translated "sum," is used in only one other place, Ezekiel 43:10, and there it is translated "pattern." Its real meaning is measure, standard, whatever is of an exact or perfect nature. The Hebrew word for seal, *chatam,* means to cut in, to impress with a seal; that is, to attest, to confirm, to verify. The phrase "thou sealest" is a participial phrase in the Hebrew, and is to be translated, "thou art the sealer of," though some ancient versions and manuscripts have "seal ring" or "signet ring" instead of sealer. In any case, the translation might properly be, "Thou art the sealer of the measure." Lange suggests accordingly, "Thou confirmedst the measure;" Young, "Thou art sealing up a measurement;" American Revised Version, margin, "Thou sealest up the sum [margin, "measure or pattern"];" the Danish has it, "Thou impresseth the seal upon the completed measure."

These different translations give the same general idea, that Lucifer had something to do with the seal, that he had the signet ring, and that that which was sealed was something perfect, a pattern, a measure. We, therefore, with the support of the original, translate: "Thou art the sealer of the measure." We take the word "measure" to denote law, a common use, as: "The legislature has just passed a new measure."

God's government is an organized government. Order exists everywhere. Nothing is left at loose ends. Each individual has his part to perform. The stars in their appointed courses, the orderly processes of nature, the uniformity of law—all testify to the existence of a Creator who is systematic, impartial, perfect.

Even as God has given each man his work to do in the evangelization of the world, so all created intelligences in the universe have their work to do. In his dream Jacob saw a ladder extending from heaven to earth, and angels ascending and descending upon it. Gen. 28:12. Zechariah saw companies of angels patrolling the earth and reporting their findings. Zech. 1:8-11. Angels were set with a sword to guard the way to the tree of life. Gen. 3:24. One angel has charge of the waters, another of the fire. Rev. 16:5; 14:18. We believe that we are correct in thinking that every angel and every created being has been given a work to do, and that in the world to come the same will be true.

The Keeper of the Seal

The highest functionary in government is the keeper of the seal. Some such position Lucifer occupied. He was one of the covering angels, one of those who had been given charge of the law, to protect it. He was the sealer, or the keeper of the seal ring that was used in confirming or attesting any ordinance or measure as it was passed. His was the highest position that any created being could occupy.

This throws light on some of Lucifer's subsequent activities. Being deprived of his office as keeper of the seal, he would naturally, as he set up his own throne, be especially interested in all that concerns the seal. That he would acquire another seal would seem most reasonable, and that this seal would be his distinguishing mark, as the seal of God had been heretofore, is also patent. Naturally, he would attempt to substitute one for the other, and each seal would respectively stand for the authority of the government concerned.

Satan "was a murderer from the beginning, and abode not in the truth." John 8:44. This text bears on the original controversy in heaven. Satan was a murderer, as well as a liar. Murder finds its origin in hatred. This hatred came to its fruition in Calvary, where Satan had an opportunity to show whom he hated. We are therefore justified in our conclusion that Satan hated Christ from the beginning, and had murder in his heart even in heaven.

What caused this hatred? The Bible gives some light on this also. Lucifer was not satisfied with the position he had. He wanted to be like God. It was this very honor which Christ was willing to relinquish. Christ was like God; He *was* God. He "thought it not robbery to be equal with God: but . . . humbled Himself." Phil. 2:6-8. The phrase "thought it not robbery" might be translated: "thought it not a thing to be grasped;" that is, thought it not a thing to be selfishly sought. Lucifer said in his heart: "I will ascend into heaven, I will exalt my throne above the stars of God: I will sit also upon the mount of

234

the congregation, in the sides of the north: I will ascend above the heights of the clouds; I will be like the Most High." Isa. 14:13, 14.

These things Lucifer "said in his heart;" that is, he thought them. But he went farther. He not only thought that he would like to be "like the Most High," but he attempted to carry this thought into effect. How far he went in this attempt we do not know, but that he tried to establish an independent government in heaven, with himself at the head, is evident. He not only planned to exalt his "throne above the stars of God," but the time came when he dared to say: "I am a God. I sit in the seat of God." Eze. 28:2. This indicates very strongly that Lucifer actually rallied around him his followers in heaven, declared himself chief, and set up his throne with the intent of ruling. He set his "heart as the heart of God." This is nothing short of rebellion. And rebellion means war.

"There was war in heaven." Rev. 12:7. With what weapons this warfare was carried on we do not presume to know. We do know that as a result "the great dragon was cast out, that old serpent, called the devil, and Satan, which deceiveth the whole world: he was cast out into the earth, and his angels were cast out with him." Rev. 12:9. We know further that "the dragon was wroth with the woman, and went to make war with the remnant of her seed, which keep the commandments of God, and have the testimony of Jesus Christ." Verse 17.

The "woman" here mentioned is the church, and the "remnant of her seed" refers to the righteous who are living just before the end. Jer. 6:2; 2 Cor. 11:2. With them Satan is wroth; that is, he hates them. This hatred is doubtless closely connected with the fact that they "keep the commandments of God, and have the testimony of Jesus."

This text is a close parallel to the statement in the fourteenth chapter of Revelation which mentions those who "keep the commandments of God, and the faith of Jesus." Verse 12. In the one text they are said to keep the commandments of God and the faith of Jesus; in the other, to keep the commandments of God and have the testimony of Jesus. The difference in the two statements is that in one they *keep* the faith of Jesus, and in the other they *have* the testimony of Jesus Christ. The "testimony of Jesus is the Spirit of prophecy." Rev. 19:10.

The dragon which makes war with the woman is "that old serpent, called the devil, and Satan." Rev. 12:9. Those against whom he makes war are the "remnant of her seed." As mentioned before, the remnant is the last church on earth, the last generation of Christians who live just before the Son of man appears in the clouds of heaven. Between them and Satan there will be war. Satan is wroth against them, and seeks to destroy them. If God did not intervene, there would be no help for them. But Christ comes to save them. He translates them to heaven, while a great angel "laid hold on the dragon, that old serpent, which is the devil, and Satan, and bound him a thousand years." Rev. 20:2. The history of this conflict is an interesting one.

The Dragon and the Woman

In the story of the Garden of Eden Satan and the first woman stood face to face. In her innocence she was overcome, and Satan gained the victory. In the last conflict, Satan again makes war with the woman. But this time the outcome is different. Satan will be defeated, and the woman will be victorious.

It has been noted already that the woman signifies the church in the vision recorded in the twelfth chapter of Revelation. While it is not the purpose to write an exhaustive explanation of this chapter, it might be well to note the main outline.

A great wonder appeared in heaven: a woman clothed with the sun, the moon under her feet, and on her head a crown of twelve stars. Verse 1. The woman was about to give birth to a child, "who was to rule all nations with a rod of iron." Verse 5. The dragon stood before her "to devour her child as soon as it was born." Verse 4. The child, however, "was caught up unto God, and to His throne." Verse 5.

The account is so plain that it needs little interpretation. The child is Christ. Evil men, led by Satan, stood ready to harm the child as soon as it was born. It became necessary for the parents to flee to Egypt, and when at last Christ's work had been accomplished, He was caught up to God and to His throne.

At first sight it would seem that according to this interpretation the woman mentioned should be the mother of Jesus, Mary. This, however, appears not to be the case. For after the child was caught up, "the woman fled into the wilderness, where she hath a place prepared of God, that they should feed her there a thousand two hundred and threescore days." Verse 6. It is generally agreed that the 1260 days here mentioned are prophetic days, each standing for a year. This of course could not be the case if Mary were meant.

But this is not the only reason for believing that the woman here mentioned is the church rather than an individual. Verse 13 states that Satan "persecuted the woman," and verse fourteen adds that to "the woman were given two wings of a great eagle, that she might fly into the wilderness, into her place, where she is nourished for a time, and times, and half a time, from the face of the serpent." The last statement in the chapter is that the dragon makes war "with the remnant of her seed, which keep the commandments of God, and have the testimony of Jesus Christ." Verse 17. This remnant, as we have noted before, is composed of the righteous in the last generation. We therefore draw the conclusion that the woman is the church of God, symbolically spoken of in this way.

In the warfare between the dragon and the woman, between evil and good, Satan can use means which give him a seeming advantage. He can use falsehoods, deception, chicanery, half truths, intimidations—none of which God's people can admit for a moment. And Satan is an expert in the use of all these. With cunning strategy his emissaries accuse God's people of their shortcomings; and these, unwilling to tell anything but the truth, confess their failings, which are immediately magnified to undue proportions by the enemy. Thus it has always been. Righteousness is made to appear sin, and sin, righteousness.

Satan never fights fairly, nor does he ever engage in open combat if he can avoid it. Hardly ever does he engage in a man-to-man encounter with equal weapons, but nearly always he attacks when his opponent is weak, sick, despondent. Nor is it a frontal attack. Generally it is a stab in the back, a poisoned arrow shot from ambush, a cowardly assassination in the dark. No sooner is the Christ child born than Satan attempts to murder Him, and mother and Child must flee to Egypt. In the wilderness, when hunger has emaciated Christ, then—and not until then—does Satan attack Him with his temptations. And so it is with everyone who tries to resist him. The one who did not hesitate to attempt to murder the helpless little Christ child, will stoop to any vile and contemptible deed. Nothing is beneath him.

The Final Controversy

The final controversy will doubtless be the crowning struggle of the ages. Satan knows that it will be his last opportunity, and that if this battle is lost, all is lost. The cunning and the wisdom he has gained through the centuries of the past will be marshaled for one supreme effort. He stakes all on the outcome.

Just what is at stake in this controversy? For Satan, everything; for God's people, everything; for God, very much. Let us study this.

God's decision not to destroy Satan after he had sinned can be defended only upon the ground that there was more at stake than merely the life of Satan. If Satan alone were to be taken into consideration, it would have been expedient to put him out of the way, the sooner the better. But there was a multitude of angels whose welfare was in jeopardy. Also, God was about to create man, and man must be taken into account. If God were to make heaven safe for all time to come, it was necessary that Satan be given permission to develop his theory of government which he claimed to be superior to God's, and demonstrate what he would do if he had the opportunity. The angels did not know Lucifer as God knew him. To avoid any possible misunderstanding in the future, God must permit Satan to establish himself and to operate a government for such as should voluntarily place themselves under his supervision. If he were permitted to do this, time would demonstrate the nature of his rule. Angels and men would have a visual demonstration of the results of following Satan, and would have ample opportunity for comparison or contrast with God's government. The experiment would give solid ground for choice, whatever the choice might be.

It has often been said, and needs to be repeated only for emphasis, that it would have been unwise for God to dispose of Satan as soon as he sinned. The other angels would henceforth have served God with a certain apprehension and fear, for they would have known that as soon as they displeased Him, they would be destroyed. Also, it might occur to them that God was afraid of Satan, of his plans and purposes, or He would have given him opportunity to demonstrate them. In any event, they would know what awaited them should they presume to deviate from God's announced will. Had Satan been killed immediately, heaven would never have been the same thereafter. The love of the angels for God would have been mixed with apprehension, and in many minds would have remained a question in regard to why Satan was not permitted to demonstrate what he had in mind.

We would not give the impression, however, that God was forced to do what He did. Rather, what He did was exactly what He wanted to do, regardless of the wishes of Satan. After sin had come, unwelcome though it was, God wanted to have its true nature revealed. He was not only willing, but anxious, that it be given full opportunity to show itself. Angels and men must have a free field of choice, and the choice, to be final and irrevocable, must be based upon a full knowledge of all the factors involved. God is not responsible for sin; but since sin has appeared, God is anxious that Satan be given a chance to show what he can do.

The deceitfulness of sin is never apparent at its inception. Sin often looks beautiful and enticing as well as innocent. Eve saw nothing wrong with the tree, or with the fruit which she had been forbidden to eat. In fact, to her it "was good," "it was pleasant," it was "to be desired." Gen. 3:6.

The end of sin is altogether different from the beginning. Eve could not understand that death was wrapped up in the eating of that fruit which looked so inviting. She did not know that as a result of sin's coming into the world through her and Adam's transgression, one of her sons would kill the other. She did not know that in seven generations man would become so corrupt that "every imagination of the thoughts of his heart" would be "only evil continually." Gen. 6:5. The fruit looked so "good;" it was "pleasant," "to be desired." Why not try it? There could certainly not be much harm in that.

Lucifer was one of the highest angels, bright, perfect in beauty, so full of wisdom that nothing could be hid from him. Eze. 28:17, 12, 3. Surely no evil could come from him. Were not even his "ways" perfect? Verse 15. Had God told the angels what Lucifer was capable of doing after he departed from the right way, it might have been hard for them to believe that God really knew. Had not Lucifer joined with them as the angelic anthems ascended in praise of their Creator? Had he not joined with them in worship and in singing, "Holy, holy, holy"? Had he not stood in the very audience chamber of God as custodian of the seal and guardian of the law? Could it be possible that such a being would rebel against God without just cause? But even if he should rebel, he would certainly never stoop to anything that in any way might be questionable, but ever would uphold the high and holy principles which he himself had helped instill in their very being.

How could the angels ever believe that Lucifer, whom they had highly revered, would harm or torture even the least of God's creatures? How could they ever believe that he would cause pain, sorrow, sickness, agony, or death? How could they ever believe that if he once got Christ in his power, he would scourge Him till the blood would run down His back, press a crown of thorns upon His brow, and drive cruel nails through His hands as he hung Him on a cross to suffer a lingering death? How could they ever believe that Lucifer would cause millions upon millions to suffer pain and excruciating agony, and many to be tortured to death by being roasted over a slow fire?

No, it would be hard for the angels to believe this. But it would be hard only because they did not know the insidious nature of sin. When at last they saw Satan do the very things here mentioned, they were overcome with the hideous, awful, revolting power of evil, and through Satan's demonstration and their reaction to it, heaven was made safe for both angels and saints. It is doubtful that it could be made safe in any other way.

The controversy, as far as human records go, has been continuing for nearly six thousand years. We are nearing the final stages. Soon will come the decisive moment upon which so much hangs. Satan has had abundant time to demonstrate what he will do if he has the opportunity. God also has been making a demonstration. The final climax is just before us.

When the end of the world is mentioned, some—and among them Christians—react unfavorably, believing that if there is such a thing as the end of the world, it is a long way off, and will not concern either them or their children. We think and believe that in many cases this is due to a misunderstanding or perhaps to lack of information. A few observations may not be amiss in regard to this important subject.

It is not our intention to enter into a full discussion of the subject of the second coming of Christ and of the end of the world. We would, however, consider it a privilege to present that phase of it which concerns us in our present discussion.

God's Suffering

However much we would like to exonerate God from any responsibility for the present world order, there are some things for which He cannot escape responsibility, and from which He does not wish to be excused. We have already discussed the matter of the imprudence of destroying Lucifer as soon as he sinned. We believe that any person who thinks the matter through will agree with this. In any event, God chose not to destroy Satan. But in choosing not to destroy him, God in reality chose to permit the present world order. While we say that God is not responsible for sin, we must at the same time admit that God permits sin. The truth is that God had power to destroy Satan, and chose not to do so. If He did not destroy him, but permitted him to continue his nefarious work, God must take the responsibility for His action. This He does.

We need not here enter into the question of how God more than nullifies the intrigues of Satan. Where sin abounds, grace does much more abound. No one needs to be deceived or lost. God "lighteth every man that cometh into the world." John 1:9. No one need be in darkness. Not only does God enlighten every man, but He makes provision for those who have been caught in the snare, so that they can escape if they wish. And this He does not only once. If a man sin a hundred times, God will forgive him. If he sin a thousand times, the door of mercy is still open. If he sin every day of his life, and live a thousand years, he may find pardon if he thoroughly repents. If he is nailed to a cross as a malefactor and deservedly is about to forfeit his life because of his crimes, there is still hope. God can do no more than He has done and is doing. If anyone is lost, it is only after God has done all in His power to avert such a tragedy, even to the offering of Himself to die in the place of the sinner. More than this no one can do.

When we speak of the sorrow and tragedy which sin has caused, and the suffering attendant upon it, we are likely to think of it only in terms of human suffering. Yet, much as mankind has suffered, God has suffered immeasurably more. It was at infinite cost to Himself that

God permitted Satan to live instead of immediately destroying him. There must be a reason for this, and this reason is found only in the unfathomable love of God. God could have saved Himself untold agony; He could have saved His Son from the cruel nails and the taunts of the wicked; He could have destroyed Satan and refused to create man; He could have done a thousand things other than what He did do, and have saved Himself from the terrific cost, to Himself, of salvation. But God did not save Himself. He so loved the world that He gave His only-begotten Son; and the Son so loved the world that He gave Himself. Much as sin has cost mankind, it has cost God a thousandfold more.

This suffering of God must be taken into account when we compute the cost both of sin and of salvation. When we hear men thoughtlessly speak of all the suffering sin has caused mankind, without taking into account the greater cost which God has paid, it is well to remember this. Some seem to think that God is far above the common experience of mankind, that He sits on a throne high and lifted up, in everlasting joy and bliss, while men are suffering the pangs of hunger and distress. Let such remember that God is touched with the feelings of our infirmities, that He "hath borne our griefs, and carried our sorrows;" that "the chastisement of our peace was upon Him; and with His stripes we are healed;" that "He was wounded for our transgressions, He was bruised for our iniquities;" that "in all their affliction He was afflicted," and that "in His love and in His pity He redeemed them;" and that because "He Himself hath suffered being tempted, He is able to succor them that are tempted;" and that "though He were a Son, yet learned He obedience by the things which He suffered." Isa. 53:4, 5; 63:9; Heb. 2:18; 5:8. In view of these statements, how can any say that God let man suffer while He Himself was unwilling to share this suffering?

While it is true that God suffers more than we, as He is higher than we are, it is nevertheless true that man suffers and has suffered long because of sin. It ought not thus ever to continue. It ought, indeed, not to continue one moment longer than is necessary. Satan's reign must be continued until he has had ample time to demonstrate what he will do and that his government is better than God's, but when the demonstration is completed, the final reckoning and assize must come. There must be a balancing of accounts, and in this angels and men are especially concerned. Satan's government and plans must be evaluated, and so must God's. In this, men and angels must have an important part.

The Lord Is Coming

Hardly anything more dreadful can be imagined than having sin and iniquity flourish forever. Some seem to think that the world is getting better, but the evidence does not support their contention. Even at this present moment men's hearts are failing them for fear of what is coming on the earth. Unless all signs earthly fail, and God's word also, we are standing on the threshold of solemn events. The end of all things is at hand. The Lord is coming, and coming soon.

A message such as this should cheer the weary heart. The coming of the Lord means the end of sin. It means the end of the great controversy. It means that God believes that Satan has at last reached the end of his demonstration, and that men and angels are ready to give their verdict. It means that the kingdoms of this world are to become the kingdoms of the Lord and of His Christ. It means that Edenic conditions will be restored, that the resurrection will take place, and that sin and sorrow will forever be of the past.

How can any Christian fail to be thrilled by such a message and by such an event? Satan has been allowed to carry on his work long enough. He must be stopped. There must be an end to sorrow and suffering. As far as we can see, if men carry on much longer, there will be no man left. Each nation—in intent at least—is getting ready to withstand every other nation. And if one nation should at last be left on the face of the earth, there is every indication that that nation would not long survive. For men with uncurbed ambition would arise in that nation, and battle to the death would be on again. No, the only solution to earth's vexing problems is the coming of the Son of man. With reverence we say that the time is near when God must intervene.

However, the Lord will not come till there has been one final demonstration both of the power of God and of the power of Satan. This is as it should be. Both God and Satan should present their finished product, that men may see and judge of the relative merits of the two antagonists. Only such a demonstration will satisfy the onlooking universe.

In Satan's first attack on the human race in the Garden of Eden, he used a serpent as the medium. In the last attack he will have recourse to a power which in the language of Revelation is called a "beast." Rev. 13:1. An "image to the beast" is also mentioned. Verse 14. This beast "had power to give life unto the image of the beast, that the image of the beast should both speak, and cause that as many as would not worship the image of the beast should be killed." Rev. 13:15. From this it can be seen that the war is one unto death. "As many as would not worship the image of the beast should be killed."

This beast "causeth all, both small and great, rich and poor, free and bond, to receive a mark in their right hand, or in their foreheads: and that no man might buy or sell, save he that had the mark, or the name of the beast, or the number of his name." Verses 16, 17.

It is significant that in this last struggle there should be reference made to a mark, and that if a man does not receive the mark, he will be able neither to buy nor to sell. We know that God's people will have a seal in their foreheads. Rev. 7:3. This seal is called "the seal of the living God." Verse 2. The 144,000 are said in the fourteenth chapter to have the Father's name written in their foreheads. Verse 1. A seal must naturally have the name of the owner of the seal engraved on it, and as this seal is the seal of the living God, we accept the view that the seal and the name of God are the same; or, rather, that the seal contains the name. In another chapter we have already discussed the seal of God, and have found that it is closely connected with the Sabbath of the Lord, that, indeed, the Sabbath is the distinguishing mark of God, that it is God's sign or seal, and that it and sanctification are inseparably connected. The reader will do well to refresh his mind by referring to the chapter "The Seal of the Law."

Sunday and Sabbath

In another chapter, "Who Changed the Sabbath?" we called attention to a power which claims not only to have changed the Sabbath from Saturday to Sunday, but also to have divine authority for doing so. And the very fact that this power has changed the Sabbath, and that the change is accepted by the Protestant church, is cited as proof of its right to change the commands of God. Can it be that this man-made sabbath is the mark of the beast, as opposed to the Sabbath of the Lord, which is the seal of God?

When Satan makes his last stand to oppose the people of God, he goes to "make war with the remnant of her seed, which keep the commandments of God, and have the testimony of Jesus Christ." Rev. 12:17. Those who thus keep the commandments have the seal of the living God in their foreheads; they have the Father's name written there. The others also have a mark in their foreheads. It does not require great insight to believe that these two marks are connected with the law of God, one as the seal of God, and the other as the mark of the apostate power.

The one great difference among Christians in regard to the law of God is in regard to the Sabbath. Some Christians keep the seventh day of the week according to the commandment. Others keep the first day. These latter are in the large majority. In order to justify their action with reference to keeping the first day, they make the claim that the law of God is abrogated and hence not binding upon Christians. They are driven to the position that the whole law is nullified rather than just one commandment—though one commandment is all they really wish to see made void—because it would seem strange to take one commandment out of the law and retain all the rest. What they do, however, is to do away with the whole law, and then re-enact the nine commandments, leaving out the offending one.

If this seems an unwarranted assertion, one need but ask a few questions. If one who observes the first day of the week were asked what he means by the statement that the law is not binding upon Christians, he would answer that as far as the Sabbath commandment is concerned, it means that he need not observe the seventh day. The commandment is no longer in force, and need not be observed. If he were asked if this applies to the whole law, he would answer that the whole law has been done away, and that we need not keep it. If he were asked to make this more specific, and apply it to a particular commandment, for example, "Thou shalt not steal," he would hardly dare take the position that a Christian need not keep that. Rather, he would say that a Christian does not and must not steal. He would take the same position with all the other commandments except the fourth. The Christian who claims that the law is abrogated, generally recedes from that position when asked to apply it to particular commandments. All he really wants and needs is to have the fourth commandment abolished, and he is willing to keep the rest.

Those who keep the seventh-day Sabbath claim to observe the law. The others indignantly repudiate the idea that they have anything to do with the law. Sabbath observance, therefore, becomes a test of a man's attitude toward the law, and toward law in general. Thus the Christian world is divided between those who keep the commandments and those who do not. The observance of the Sabbath constitutes the dividing line.

It is on this battle front that the last struggle will be fought. Satan goes to "make war with the remnant of her seed, which keep the commandments of God, and have the testimony of Jesus Christ." This means that they keep all the commandments, and that this is what makes Satan angry.

It should not be thought, however, that the struggle is confined to the mere matter of a day; that is, whether the seventh day or the first day is the one to be kept. There is more involved than that. The roots of the controversy lie much deeper. They touch the question of evolution, of inspiration, of the integrity of the word of God, of Modernism or Fundamentalism, of the plan of salvation, of the sacrifice of the cross, of the government of God itself. The final choice made in view of these considerations decides the destiny of man and of mankind.

Martin Luther

Four hundred years ago a young monk decided to take his stand by the word of God, whatever the cost. Tradition had been his guide, but henceforth the word of God, and the word of God only, would be his lodestar. Whether he ever said the words attributed to him or not, the sentiment is surely his, and that of a large body of Christians today: "Here I stand, I can do no other; may God help me." "Here I stand," he said, placing his hand on the Bible. And "the Bible, and the Bible only," has from that time been the rallying cry of true Protestants. When that ceases to be the truth, Protestantism ceases to be.

We are today witnessing the disintegration of the movement that began so nobly in Germany four hundred years ago. Many of these who have stood for the faith once delivered to the saints, who raised the cry, "Back to the Bible!" have deserted the cause and are among the foremost in dissecting the precious volume of God. It is not the atheists, it is not the infidels, it is not the Mohammedans, it is not the Catholics, who bear major responsibility for destroying reverence for the Bible and making it of none effect. It is the Protestant clergy who are undermining the foundations.

It is in the theological seminaries in which the clergy are educated that the chief work is being done. One after another of these former strongholds is deserting its original position and breaking down that which it formerly built up. There are not many colleges of first rank that remain true to the faith of the fathers. Most of them are honeycombed with Modernism, not to say skepticism; and the sturdy faith of the teachers who once taught in their halls is largely nonexistent. Protestantism was built on the Bible as its foundation. We submit that it is not possible to remove the foundation and expect the superstructure to stand.

If the sixteenth century needed a voice to call men to the Bible, the twentieth century needs a still stronger voice. The Protestant movement as such seems doomed.

There is hardly a church that bears the name "Protestant" which does not have ministers and teachers who openly proclaim the fallibility of revelation, the errancy of Scripture, and the inadequacy of blood atonement. If the church continues for a few more years in the direction it is now going, common honesty will demand that the name "Protestant" be dropped, and a name more in harmony with facts be substituted. What form the new movement will take we are not prepared to say, but it will be Protestant no more.

Does this mean, then, that the work so nobly begun a few hundred years ago shall come to nought? We believe not. God was in that movement. Its fault was that it was not continued beyond the lifetime of its founders. No man knows all truth. God's revelation is not communicated all at once. It is here a little, there a little, line upon line, precept upon precept. A steady walking in the light would have brought newer and greater revelations, and saved some from the pitfalls into which they fell.

There is no way in which a movement founded upon the Bible, and upon the Bible only, can accept the traditions of men in preference to the word of God. As soon as it does so, it ceases to be a Bible movement, and fails to the extent to which it departs from Bible truth. When this happens, God gives time for repentance; but if there is no repentance, God will raise up another people to finish the work begun, and to carry it on to greater success. The Protestant church may cease to be, but Protestantism will continue.

God has not left this world, nor is He satisfied with half measures. If the church fails in an hour such as this, God has means at hand that will restore the old faith. There are those who will build the old waste places, raise up the foundations of many generations, repair the breach, and restore the paths to dwell in. God does not leave Himself without a witness. Men may depart from the law, they may hew themselves cisterns which will hold no water, they may consider themselves wise above what is written, but God's arm is not shortened. He has in reserve instruments whom men may despise, but who nevertheless will cause God's name to be known to the ends of the earth. God knows what He is doing. And He knows them that are His.

We believe that the time has come for a new Protestant movement, one that will rally Bible believers in all churches and societies, and unite them in one body for the defense of the faith. Men have made void the law of God. It is time for Him to work. From one end of the earth to the other the call must sound. Protestantism has deserted its standards. A new Protestantism must arise.

One Fold, One Shepherd

Christ's word, "There shall be one fold, and one Shepherd," will yet be fulfilled before the end. John 10:16. There are now many folds, and honest believers in all of them. This shall not always thus continue. The call will sound: "Come out of her, My people, that ye be not partakers of her sins, and that ye receive not of her plagues." Rev. 18:4. God will gather His own into one fold, and when the final struggle comes, there will be no doubt in regard to where each stands. The people thus called out will keep the commandments of God and the faith of Jesus. Rev. 14:12.

The question may be asked if it is possible to unite all the true saints of God in one body. Which creed will be accepted? What unifying factor is there to be to bind them together? With the many different denominations now in existence, is it not too much to believe that there could ever be a call sounded that would be strong enough to draw these diverse elements into one body?

Says Christ: "Other sheep I have, which are not of this fold: them also I must bring, and they shall hear My voice; and there shall be one fold, and one Shepherd." John 10:16. Note: "They shall hear My voice." As the Good Shepherd, Christ goes before the sheep. They follow Him. In these few words Christianity is summed up. "He goes before them, and the sheep follow Him: for they know His voice." Verse 4. Christianity is just that simple. To follow Christ is all the theology anyone needs for salvation. On that platform all Christians can unite. And as one follows Christ, and another follows Him, the two will walk together. And as all follow Him, there will be one fold and one Shepherd.

Will this ever come to fruition in this earth? We believe so. As the nominal churches depart more and more from the faith of the living God, there will be those in every communion who are longing for a consolation in Israel. They will see hundreds of churches with thousands of believers, each church different in faith from the others, and yet with people in it who are truly trying to serve God. They will be perplexed, and will wonder what they are to do and what they are to believe. One great man of the church will say one thing, and another equally great will say something different. In his perplexity the true child of God will turn to the Word, and it will suddenly dawn upon him, as though it were a new revelation, that Christ is the way, the truth, and the light, and that all he needs to do is to follow Him, and every religious problem will be solved. Breaking with every earthly tie, men will set out to follow the Lamb whithersoever He leadeth, and to their astonishment will find that others are pursuing the same course. On the simple program and creed of following the Lamb, they will unite in divine fellowship, and God will set His seal of approval upon them. They follow the Lamb; they have the Father's name written upon their foreheads; the Lord owns them as His; they are sealed for eternity.

When men follow this simple program, there will be developed a people who will keep the commandments of God, and the faith of Jesus. Jesus states definitely: "I have kept My Father's commandments." John 15:10. Those who follow Jesus will keep the commandments. If any do not, it simply shows that they do not follow Him.

We are therefore safe in believing that there will be a return to primitive faith and godliness before the coming of the Son of man. Men will begin to follow the Master again, trustfully doing what He did. With apostolic faith will come apostolic power. The whole world will be arraigned in two camps: those who keep the commandments of God and the faith of Jesus, and those who do not. There will be no mistaking the saints. They will have the seal of the living God in their foreheads.

Of all the experiences through which the saints go, the Sabbath is a sign. Believing in the simple story of creation as recorded in the first chapters of Genesis, they will naturally accept the account of the Sabbath. The two go together. Believing in Christ, they will follow Him and accept Him as the way, the truth, and the life. Accepting Christ as their Lord, they accept Him also as the Lord of the Sabbath. As He rested, so do they rest. They follow Him whithersoever He goeth.

It is against this company that the wrath of Satan will be directed. It is against them that he will make war. And the struggle will be fierce in its intensity. The decree will at last be issued that whoever will not worship according to the command of the "beast" shall be killed. Rev. 13:15. Then comes the time of Jacob's trouble. Satan is determined to test the people of God to the utmost, and if possible, to make them sin. If he succeeds, he has gained an important point, for God has determined to show His power in this very people. In and through them He intends to give a demonstration to the world of what the gospel can do for humanity.

The last generation of men carry all the sins and the weaknesses of their forefathers. If any are weak, they are. If any have inherited or cultivated tendencies to evil, they have. If it is possible for *them* to live through the struggles of the last days without sinning, it has always been possible to live sinlessly. And this is the very thing which God intends to demonstrate through them. This demonstration will also settle the question whether it is possible for men to keep the law. If these people can do so, it is conclusively proved that man *can* keep the law, and that God is not unjust in requiring obedience.

The last generation of God's people, therefore, constitutes a special company. Satan is given permission to try them to the utmost. He makes war against them. He threatens them. They are under death sentence. But all these things do not move them. "Here is the patience of the saints." They endure, they continue steadfast, they are immovable. Threats and flatteries fall on deaf ears. All that Satan can do is without effect. They, as did Christ, go through Gethsemane. And as He came out victorious, so do these. When the struggle is over, they are seen standing on Mount Zion, with the Father's name written in their foreheads. They are without fault before the throne of God.

In these 144,000 God stands justified. He has proved by them that the law can be kept under the most adverse circumstances. He has disproved Satan's assertion that God is unjust in demanding that men keep the law. God is vindicated. Satan is defeated. The controversy is ended. All that remains is the balancing of accounts. And then—after the judgment is ended—comes the reign of God, unending, glorious. God speed that day!

We'd love to have you download our catalog of titles we publish or even hear your thoughts, reactions, or criticism about this or any other book we publish at:

www.TEACHServices.com
or
info@TEACHServices.com

Or call us at:

518/358-3494